¡Uno, dos, tres!

Upper Juniors
Years 5-6

Eileen Jones

Published by Hopscotch,
a division of MA Education,
St Jude's Church, Dulwich Road,
London, SE24 0PB
www.hopscotchbooks.com
020 7738 5454

©2015 MA Education Ltd.

Written by Eileen Jones

Designed by Fonthill Creative, 01722 717057

Illustrated by Emma Turner

ISBN 978-1-909860-278

All rights reserved. This resource is sold subject to the condition that it shall not, by way of trade or otherwise, be lent, hired out or otherwise circulated without the publisher's prior consent in any form of binding or cover other than that in which it is published and without a similar condition, including this condition, being imposed upon the subsequent purchaser.

No part of this publication may be reproduced, stored in a retrieval system, or transmitted, in any form or by any means, electronic, mechanical, photocopying, recording or otherwise, without the prior permission of the publisher, except where photocopying for educational purposes within the school or other educational establishment that has purchased this book is expressly permitted in the text.

Every effort has been made to trace the owners of copyright of material in this book and the publisher apologises for any inadvertent omissions. Any persons claiming copyright for any material should contact the publisher who will be happy to pay the permission fees agreed between them and who will amend the information in this book on any subsequent reprint.

contents

Introduction 6

Unit thirteen – **¡Que aproveche!** *(Enjoy your meal!)* 7

Unit fourteen – **Yo soy músico** *('I am the music man')* 14

Unit fifteen – **Vamos al colegio** *(On the way to school)* 21

Unit sixteen – **Una escena de la playa** *(Beach scene)* 27

Unit seventeen – **Los cuatro estaciones** *(The four seasons)* 34

Unit eighteen – **Los planetas** *(The planets)* 41

Unit nineteen – **Nuestro colegio** *(Our school)* 49

Unit twenty – **Nuestro mundo** *(Our world)* 56

Unit twenty-one – **Crear una cafetería** *(Creating a café)* 63

Unit twenty-two – **El pasado y el presente** *(Then and now)* 70

Unit twenty-three – **En el parque de atracciones** *(At the theme park)* 77

Unit twenty-four – **¿Qué noticias hay?** *(What's in the news?)* 84

Introduction

About the book
¡Uno, dos, tres! aims to make Spanish practical and achievable. Its exciting and appropriate material will ensure that children of all levels of ability have the opportunities to both enjoy and achieve in their language learning. It will support you, whatever your level of linguistic confidence or competence.

This book builds on the teaching of Book 1 (Lower Juniors). It continues to address three fundamental strands of language teaching: oracy, literacy and intercultural understanding. It responds to the recommendations of the National Curriculum for Foreign Languages by providing opportunities for the children to:

- become increasingly familiar with the sounds and written form of Spanish;

- make comparisons between Spanish and other languages;

- expand their cultural awareness;

- grow in confidence as they understand what they hear and read;

- learn to communicate;

- develop linguistic competence;

- present ideas orally to a range of audiences;

- describe people, places, things and actions orally and in writing;

- understand basic grammar appropriate to the language being studied.

Using the book
Reflecting the structure of the National Curriculum for Foreign Languages, the book is divided into twelve Units. Each Unit forms the basis of half a term's work and covers a theme that crosses cultures and is relevant to the children's lives. For each Unit, there is an introduction stating the main teaching points, grammar, language sounds, and vocabulary to be addressed. There are four, easy-to-follow, fully planned and resourced, ready-to-use lessons. These are supported by photocopiable worksheets and follow-up ideas. Each lesson plan explains what you will need, how to prepare, what to say to the children and what to encourage them to say.

Make one lesson the core of a week's teaching. Keep returning to the contents of a lesson during the week, playing, repeating and adapting games, so you give all the children the confidence to contribute. Use the Follow-up activity as a tool for differentiation, only more able children completing the full task. Teach the lessons in chronological order, so learning in one is a foundation for the next. Finally, draw the Unit together with the 'More ideas' section of school and home activities, using the section to revise and consolidate the lessons' main teaching points and extend opportunities to learn about Spanish culture.

The main aim of language teaching is to develop linguistic competence, so be ready to adapt material to suit your opportunities. A game used in one Unit may be adapted easily to consolidate learning in another Unit. Similarly, grasp opportunities to take Spanish beyond timetabled lessons and into other areas of classroom life. Most of all, generate enthusiasm, as children gain pleasure from their language-learning skills.

> Spain is the third largest country in Europe and has an area of 504,782 sq km. It is over twice as big as the United Kingdom!

Unit 13 – ¡Que aproveche!

(Enjoy your meal!)

Unit theme
Food and drink

Teaching points
- Talking about what has been eaten or drunk
- Expressing likes, dislikes and preferences about food and drink
- Understanding and giving instructions
- Following and writing instructions (recipes)

Grammar
- Preterite tense: *comer (comí) beber (bebí)*
- Plural nouns with *los/las*; *unos/unas*
- Compound sentences with connectives *y* and *pero*
- Agreement of adjectives: masculine and feminine, singular and plural
- Imperatives: *tú* form of regular and irregular verbs

Language sounds
- *a*

Vocabulary

Comí	I ate
Bebí	I drank
¿Comiste (un plátano)?	Did you eat (a banana)?
y	and
pero	but
Prefiero	I prefer
¿Prefieres…?	Do you prefer?
un bocadillo	a sandwich
un pastel	a cake
un plátano	a banana
una pizza	a pizza
queso (m)	(some) cheese
agua (f)	(some) water
zumo de naranja (m)	orange juice
patatas fritas (f plural)	(some) crisps or chips
un paquete de patatas fritas	a packet of crisps
un zumo de naranja (m)	an orange juice
la salsa de caramelo	toffee sauce
el pan	bread
una rebanada de pan	a slice of bread
un pan de pita	a pitta bread
el berro	watercress
champiñones (m)	mushrooms
queso rallado (m)	grated cheese
el pescado	fish
el chocolate	chocolate
los caramelos (m)	sweets
el yogurt	yoghurt
la coca	cola
las zanahorias (f)	carrots
una manzana	an apple
un tomate	a tomato
una judía	a bean
Es bueno/buena para la salud	It's good for your health
Es malo/mala para la salud	It's bad for your health
Son buenos/buenas/ malos/malas para la salud	They're good/bad for your health

(Instructions are given in the familiar form)

Pon	Put
Añade	Add
Corta	Cut
Calienta	Heat up
Haz	Make
¡Comí!	Eat!
una bandeja de horno	a baking tray
el horno	the oven

Additional vocabulary for teachers

¿Te gustan (los plátanos)?	Do you like (bananas)?
¿Tienes (un plátano)?	Have you got (a banana)?
¿Bebiste (agua)?	Did you drink water?

Resources
Food and food pictures

¡Uno, dos, tres!

Lesson 1 ¿Qué tienes? (What have you got?)

Resources:
Food pictures or props; six small lunch boxes; a feely bag of plastic (or real) fruit and vegetables; one copy of photocopiable 6A, Book 1 (Lower Juniors)

- Display pictures of foods already taught. How many names can partners tell each other? Revise known foods and drinks suitable for a snack. For example: *un zumo de naranja* (an orange juice), *una manzana* (an apple), *los caremelos* (sweets), *las zanahorias* (carrots). Share results, turning over the pictures to check.

- Say and write new foods: *un plátano* (a banana), *un bocadillo,* (a sandwich), *el queso* (cheese), *un paquete de patatas fritas* (crisps), the children repeating them after you. Highlight and practise the pronunciation of *a* in *manzana, me gusta, naranja, plátano*.

- Draw attention to the meaning of *una/una* (a, an) and *unos/unas* (some). Explain that the equivalent of the English word 'any' is usually left out in Spanish, for example: *¿Tienes agua?* (Do you have any water?)

- Select a list of 8-10 appropriate snack foods to leave on the whiteboard. Give everyone a piece of card to choose and write one of them for their snack.

- Arrange the children in a large circle and play **La ensalada mixta** (mixed salad):

  ○ Call out a food name: those children change places.

  ○ Call out two food names: those children may change places.

  ○ Call out *La ensalada mixta*: anyone may change places with someone.

  ○ After two or three minutes of playing, check how mixed your salad is!

- Put the children into groups of four to six to share food information as they question and answer one another:

  ○ *¿Qué tienes?* (What have you got?)

  ○ *Tengo…* (I have…)

- Ask everyone to hold up a food. Ask *¿Que tienes?* In reply, a child should say *Tengo… un bocadillo*.

- Ask the children to draw something they ate yesterday. Introduce present and past tense verbs: *Como* (I am eating) *Comí* (I ate); *Bebo* (I am drinking) *Bebí (*I drank*)*. Pretend to eat and say *Como un bocadillo* (I am eating a sandwich.) Take a step backwards, as if in time, and say *Ayer comí un bocadillo* (Yesterday I ate a sandwich). Do the same with a drink: *Bebo un zumo de naranja* (I am drinking an orange juice) and *Ayer bebí un zumo de naranja* (Yesterday I drank an orange juice).) Emphasise that the past tense forms of verbs are used when talking about things that have already happened. Practise them as a whole class, children using the present and past verbs with the food or drink they are holding.

- Give each group a snack box and explain **Carry-on!**

  ○ One group member puts his food in the snack box and says *Tengo…* (+ the name of his food). The box passes to the next person, who, having added her food to the box, repeats what the first person said and the name of her food. So the box gets fuller and the chant gets longer. (Children may find it easier to speak as a group, individuals only saying alone their food name.)

  ○ Listen to every group's packed lunch box. Vote on which sounds tastiest.

- Finish by playing **Feel around**. Give partners a 10 second feel of your prepared feely bag of plastic fruit and vegetables. Ask *¿Que tienes en la bolsa? (*What do you have in the bag?) The class replies *En la bolsa tengo…* and partners say one food they think they have identified. After every pair has had a turn, how many of your secret foods have the children discovered?

Follow-up
Suggest making a morning snack timetable, the children drawing and labelling their planned snacks for the school week.

Lesson 2 ¿Es bueno para la salud? (Is it good for your health?)

Resources:
Food pictures or props from Lesson 1; photocopiable 13A

- Revise and introduce food vocabulary by showing pictures or props.

- Bring out a container labelled *Es bueno para la salud*. Confirm the meaning. (It is good for your health.)

- Ask the children to help you identify healthy foods. Agree on a healthy sign (for example, a thumbs up). Say only <u>singular masculine</u> foods, for example: *el pastel, el queso, un pan de pita, el chocolate*. When the children make the agreed sign, help them say their verdict in a sentence, for example: *Un bocadillo es bueno para la salud. El pastel no es bueno para la salud.*

- Use a singular feminine noun in the same sentence construction. For example: *Una manzana es buena para la salud*. Display the written sentences. Can the children spot an important spelling difference? (*bueno* has become *buena*) Confirm the feminine agreement between the noun and the adjective.

- Announce a hearing test! Give everyone two hearing cards, *bueno* and *buena*. (Some children may prefer to work with a partner, one card each). Read out assorted masculine and feminine sentences, for example: *El chocolate no es bueno para la salud. Una zanahoria es buena para la salud.* Stop after each for the children to hold up a card. Confirm if they are correct. After 10 sentences, how many hearing points did they get? Does their hearing need a re-test?

- Give further practice in adjective agreement by repeating the previous teaching activities for the adjective forms *malo* and *mala*.

- Remind the children about the conjunctions *y* (and) and *pero* (but). Demonstrate their use to form a longer, compound sentence from two short sentences: *Me gusta la tomate y ella es buena para la salud. Me gusta el chocolate pero él no es bueno para la salud. Me gusta una tomate pero prefiero un plátano.*

- Divide the class into three groups **A**, **B** and **C**. Set these tasks:

  ○ **Group A**: children write a short sentence beginning *Me gusta....* and complete it with a food.

  ○ **Group B**: children write a short food sentence beginning *Él es...* or *Ella es....* and complete it with a comment about whether it is healthy.

  ○ **Group C**: children work with a partner, making and writing two conjunction cards, *y* and *pero*.

- Ask **A** children to find a **B** sentence that matches their noun, the new partners then searching for the **C** conjunction they think will suit them. (Have a supply of spare **B** sentences and **C** conjunctions.)

- Challenge each new **A B C** group to join up into a compound sentence, standing in order as they say their sentence to the class. Does the class agree with the choice of conjunction?

Follow-up
Give the children photocopiable 13A to complete, reminding them of the use of the pronouns *él/ella* (it) and the plural *ellos/ellas* (they) to replace nouns and the need for adjectives and nouns or pronouns to agree.

Lesson 3 La Fiesta de San Fermín (The San Fermín festival)

Resources:
Access to the Internet

- Make sure the days of the week and months of the year are on prominent display.

- Put the children into teams of three to play **Make a date**. Allocate roles: one person the day, one the date, the third person the month.

- Call out a date, for example *lunes, tres de julio*, (Monday, July 3) for team members to write their part on their individual whiteboard and quickly stand in the correct order. Award team points to the correct human dates made in the time allowed.

- As the children improve, reduce the time allowed or award points to only the first three correct teams.

- Explain the significance of the first week in July in the Spanish city of Pamplona:

  ○ it is the date of the San Fermín fiesta;

  ○ this is an annual bull-running festival;

  ○ bulls run along the street to the bullring every morning;

  ○ brave, fit, fast people run in front of them for part of the way!

- Emphasise the importance of food, bonfires and fireworks as part of the celebration of San Fermín.

- Let the children work with a partner to list in Spanish about six fun foods that will suit an evening bonfire and fireworks party for either our Bonfire Night or Spain's San Fermín fiesta.

Follow-up
Ask the children to make a poster advertising a bonfire celebration, drawing and labelling (in Spanish) the food that will be available. Suggest putting an English flag on one half of the poster and a Spanish flag on the other to emphasise the link between the two countries' celebrations.

Lesson 4 ¡Un bocadillo delicioso! (A delicious sandwich!)

Resources:
Food pictures or props; individual copies of photocopiable 13B

- Remind the children about the importance of food in Spanish leisure time. Explain that families often enjoy picnics at the weekend.

- Invite the children to play **Simon dice** (Simon says) as they mime getting food ready. Use these verbs in your instructions: *pon, añade, corta, calienta*. For example: *Corta un tomate*; *Pon queso en un bocadillo*; *Añade el jamón*. Remind the children that they should only mime if you begin with *Simon dice*.

- Write the heading *Se necesita* (What is needed), display pictures and say the ingredients for a toasted cheese and ham sandwich: *el pan, queso rallado, el jamón*. (bread, grated cheese, ham). Read out your recipe's instructions, using action and mime to clarify meanings:

Instrucciones

○ **Corta** *dos rebanadas de pan.*

○ **Pon** *queso en el pan.*

○ **Añade** *el jamón.*

○ **Haz** *un bocadillo.*

○ **Calienta** *el bocadillo.*

○ *¡Comí!*

- Repeat the instructions, this time the children miming the actions.

- Write the whole recipe, including the headings (*Se necesita* and *ingredientes* and *Instrucciones*) on the whiteboard. Can the children identify the verb forms highlighted? Point out their position at the start of sentences and their role of giving commands. Guide the children to identifying them as imperatives.

- Pretend it is the family picnic! Give the children permission to create their own *bocadillo*. With sweet or savoury ingredients, it does not have to be healthy!

- Let the children plan their ideas, using bilingual dictionaries to list their ingredients.

Follow-up
Give the children photocopiable 13B to complete, suggesting they first write their recipe in rough. Encourage helpful illustrations and inventive sandwich names. Afterwards, use the recipes to compile a class cookery book.

There are wonderful nightly fireworks displays as part of the San Fermín festival in Pamplona.

¡Uno, dos, tres!

¡Que approveche!

adjectives	adjectives	conjunctions
bueno	malo	y
buena	mala	pero
buenos	malos	
buenas	malas	

Part 1

For sentences labelled **a**, fill the gap with the correct food noun.

For sentences labelled **b**, choose the adjective to agree with the noun.

1a Me gusta la – _____
 b Ella es – para la salud.

2a Me gusta el – _____
 b Él es – para la salud.

3a Me gusta el– _____
 b Él es – para la salud.

4a No me gusta el – _____
 b Él es – para la salud.

5a Me gustan los – _____
 b Ellos son – para la salud.

6a No me gustan las – _____
 b Ellas son – para la salud.

Part 2

Make one sentence from each pair of sentences, using the conjunction **y** or **pero**.

Se necesita

Instrucciones

More ideas for...

Work at school

- Make **Carry-on!** (Lesson 1) into a regular favourite by organising quick games. They will extend the children's food vocabulary and improve their confidence as speakers.

- Suggest the children make a bilingual food dictionary. Encourage them to think carefully about how to organise it for easy reference. Will illustrations help? Will computer presentation make it easier to add new words? What about alphabetical order?

- Use the data collected in the **Follow-up** activity to Lesson 1 for the children, with the help of a partner, to award between one and five *¡Para la salud!'* (Healthy!) stars to each of their snacks. Suggest the children total their stars. Use an ICT lesson for the children to present the data in graphical representation. (They could combine information with a partner.) Afterwards ask them to interpret the graphs. What facts are shown about their eating habits? Is one day particularly likely to be unhealthy?

- Put the children into small groups and provide the ingredients to follow the recipe in Lesson 4. Use a sandwich-maker to toast each sandwich. Afterwards ask the children to write about their reactions to making and tasting it. Provide sentences ideas, for example:

    Me gusta/No me gusta el bocadillo. Él es... delicioso/horrible. Él es fácil/difícil de hacer.

Work at home

- Set a research task for the children to discover more about the San Fermín festival celebrations.

- Challenge the children to find out about the food *Pan con tomate*.

- Ask the children to make an illustrated menu showing *Pan con tomate* and a toasted sandwich. Underneath they should write which they prefer. (*Prefiero ...*) Can they persuade their parents to let them help make it?

- Give the children photocopiable 13B, a list of useful imperative verbs and food vocabulary (perhaps their food dictionaries from **Work at school**) to take home. Ask them to create a recipe for a salad (fruit or vegetable), try it out, and write a rough draft before they complete photocopiable 13B.

Pamplona is a Spanish city full of history and deep-rooted traditions. It was founded by Pompey, the Roman general, in 75BC.

Unit 14 – Yo soy músico

('I am the music man')

Unit theme
Responding to music

Teaching points
- Offering opinions (about music)
- Making simple statements (about musical instruments)
- Expressing future intentions (about playing a musical instrument)

Grammar
- *Tocar* + *el/la/los/las* (with a musical instrument)
- Immediate future: *ir* + infinitive (*Voy a tocar; Voy a cantar*)

Language sounds
- Syllable stress

Vocabulary

un saxofón	a saxophone
un piano	a piano
un violín	a violin
un clarinete	a clarinet
una guitarra	a guitar
una trompeta	a trumpet
la batería	the drums
las castañuelas (f plural)	castanets
Voy a tocar el/la …	I am going to play the …
Voy a cantar	I am going to sing
¡Es fantástico/a!	It's fantastic!
¡Es malísimo/a/horrible/aburrido/a!	It's rubbish/awful/boring!
la música jazz	jazz music
la música reggae	reggae music
la música pop	pop music
la música clásica	classical music
la música folclórica	folk music
la música inglesa, española, (latino) americana, africana	English, Spanish, (Latin) American, African music

Additional vocabulary for teachers

¿Qué tipo de música es?	What kind of music is it?
¿Qué vas a hacer?	What are you going to do?
Hay…	There is…/There are …
Cambiad/cambia el ritmo	Change (plural/singular) the beat
¿Cuántos ritmos hay?	How many beats are there?
¡Buena suerte!	Good luck!

Resources
Separate pieces of music: at least one example of classical, jazz, folk, reggae, pop)
Musical instruments (or pictures)

¡Uno, dos, tres!

Lesson 1 ¡Es la música! (It's music!)

Resources:
Separate pieces of music to listen to with at least one example of each style: classical, jazz, folk, reggae, pop

- Tell the children to prepare for a musical extravaganza!

- Write these five style names on the whiteboard: *la música jazz*; *la música reggae*; *la música pop*; *la música clásica*; *la música folclórica*. Read them aloud for the children to repeat. Can they guess the meanings?

- Give everyone a piece of paper divided into five squares. Play the pieces of music, pausing after each for partners to hold whispered discussions about which style they think has just been played.

- Re-play the music pieces in the same order, pausing after each for the children to write a style's name.

- Confirm answers and find out who are the music experts!

- Bring out Juan, your class puppet, and ask him: *¿Te gusta la música pop?* (Do you like pop music?) Disguising your voice, answer for him: *Sí, me gusta la música pop.* Use the same question format to ask him about *la música clásica*, answering *No me gusta la música clásica*.

- Let the children question a partner about their music tastes, always beginning *¿Te gusta … ?*

- Revise the connectives *y* and *pero* (Unit 13, Lesson 2). Write Juan's two answers on the whiteboard and suggest creating one sentence. Which connective would be better? (*pero*) Demonstrate with *Me gusta la música pop pero no me gusta la música clásica*.

Follow-up
Using the last sentence as a model, let the children write a two-part sentence about their music tastes, using *Me gusta …* and *no me gusta* (or *prefiero*)… and connecting with *pero*. When they read their sentence to a partner, are there any surprises?

Lesson 2 ¡Toco el piano! (I play the piano)

Resources:
These musical instruments (or pictures): saxophone, piano, violin, guitar, clarinet, drums

- Take the class to the music room and show them these instruments: saxophone, piano, violin, guitar, clarinet, drums. (Alternatively, use pictures.)

- Put Spanish labels by the instruments and model saying them.

- Make the names familiar by playing these variations of **What's my name?**

    ○ Collect instrument labels so the class can help you re-place them.

    ○ Collect and shuffle labels for individual children to pick and place one.

    ○ Let the class vote with their *sí* or *no* card if the label is placed correctly.

    ○ Mix up the labels, when the children's eyes are shut. Challenge a group to sort and place them within a time limit. Which group beats the clock?

    ○ Say an instrument name for the children to represent it with the appropriate playing action.

    ○ Hold up a label for the children to read aloud and point to the correct instrument.

- Play **Charades**, everyone secretly choosing an instrument to play in the orchestra. Choose someone to mime playing. Choose someone to ask the guessing question, for example: *¿Tocas … el clarinette?* If correct, the miming player replies *Sí, toco el clarinette*. If incorrect, someone else asks the guessing question. Keep the game going with new players chosen to mime.

- Play the separate music extracts from Lesson 1. Provide the construction *Hay…* as the children write a sentence for each, identifying an instrument they can hear. For example: *1. Hay una guitarra*.

Follow-up
Use a simple tune for *¡Toco el piano!* on photocopiable 14A. Divide the class into four groups and share out verses 2-5 to practise. Hold a class performance, everyone singing verses 1 and 6, separate groups singing and making appropriate playing actions and sounds for their verse.

Lesson 3 ¿Cuántos ritmos hay? (How many beats are there?)

Resources:
Photocopiable 14A; individual copies of the interview form in **Follow-up**

- Give the instruction *Battez la mesure* for the children to clap a beat.

- Hold another performance of *¡Toco el piano!* (Photocopiable 14), the children joining you in clapping the beat. Between verses, alter the tempo with the instruction *Cambiad el ritmo*. Encourage the group that is singing to match the beat.

- Revise vocabulary as you ask children questions such as these:

  ○ *¿Cómo te llamas? (Me llamo … Juan.)*

  ○ *¿Te gusta la música jazz?*

  ○ *¿Tocas el saxofón?*

  ○ *¿Te gusta la música clásica?*

  ○ *¿Prefieres la música pop?*

- Explain that you will be holding a music contest, and are interviewing music groups to enter. Share and list on the whiteboard suggestions for group names, for example: *¡Los músicos fantásticos!* (The fantastic musicians!) *¡Los músicos distintos!* (The different players!) *Los leones* (The lions).

- Put the children into music groups of five to decide on their name and who will play which instrument. Suggest making notes, in Spanish when possible, of their decisions.

- Warn them that you, as interviewer, will expect them all to speak! You may ask their name, their musical taste, what instrument they will play in the group, and the group's name. On the whiteboard, write sample questions and answer openers (See **Follow-up** and the vocabulary list on the Unit's opening page) so the children can prepare by doing partner conversations.

- Use Juan, your class puppet, to demonstrate asking and answering a question about their future playing: *¿Qué vas a hacer? (Voy a tocar el saxofón.)*

- During conversation practice, move among groups, prompting ideas, adding vocabulary and guiding sentences.

- Hold the interviews (the class listening to each in turn). Announce your decision: every group has passed! They will all be in the music contest!

Follow-up
Create and print individual copies of this interview form. Let the children take turns interviewing a partner before they write their own answers:

○ *¡Buenos días!*
_____

○ *¿Cómo te llamas?*
_____

○ *¿Y el grupo?*
_____

○ *¿Te gusta la música jazz?*
_____

○ *¿Prefieres la música pop?*
_____

○ *¿Qué vas a hacer?*
_____

○ *¡Buena suerte!*
_____

Lesson 4 ¡El rap! (Rap!)

Resources:
Photocopiable 14B

- Remind the children about the forthcoming music contest and form the groups from Lesson 3. Use questions, for example those from Lesson 3's **Follow-up**, to revise group names and musician roles.

- Give the children photocopiable 14B and read and translate the words. Do a performance of the rap together.

- Suggest the rap needs one or two additional verses before finishing with a repetition of the first verse. The contest task is to compose and perform the extra verses!

- As groups compose, move among them, helping with vocabulary; suggest the use of word banks and dictionaries; and point out that poetic licence may allow them to omit a word (for example, *el*) to maintain the rhythm. Make sure that each group's organisation gives everyone involvement. (A group may work as a whole, or allocate some lines to some members.) Word processing will make drafting and editing words easier.

- When verses are written, find an appropriate space, perhaps the hall, for group rehearsals.

- Stage the contest! Make a recording as each group performs in turn, the rest of you listening and applauding. Encourage a positive attitude, as members of the audience make a secret note of their reaction to the rap and a score.

- At the end of the contest, hold a secret ballot and announce the winning group.

Follow-up

Display the words of the winning rap for a class performance. Find an occasion, perhaps a class assembly, for a performance for the school. Make a recording of the rap to exchange with a partner school's music. Consider putting material on the school's website.

¡Yo toco el piano!

1   Yo soy músico
Y toco el piano.
Pia-pia-piano, piano, piano
Pia-pia-piano, piano, piano.
¡Yo toco el piano!

2   Yo soy músico
Y toco el violín.
Vio-vio-violín, violín, violín
Vio-vio-violín, violín, violín.
¡Yo toco el violín!

3   Yo soy músico
Y toco el clarinete.
Clari-clari-clarinete, clarinete, clarinete
Clari-clari-clarinete, clarinete, clarinete.
¡Yo toco el clarinete!

4   Yo soy músico
Y toco la batería.
Bater-bater- batería, batería, batería
Bater-bater- batería, batería, batería.
¡Yo toco la batería!

5   Yo soy músico
Y toco el saxofón.
Saxo-saxo-saxofón
Saxo-saxo-saxofón
¡Yo toco el saxofón!

6   Yo soy músico
Y toco el piano.
Pia-pia-piano, piano, piano
Pia-pia-piano, piano, piano.
¡Yo toco el piano!

El rap

*Así que hoy
Hacemos un rap.
¡Es muy fácil!
Hacemos un rap.*

*En primer lugar,
Hay las palabras.
En segundo lugar.
Hay el ritmo.*

*Uno, dos, tres, cuatro
Hacen el ritmo.
¿Vas a cambiar?
¡No, él es bueno!*

*¡Escribid! ¡Escribid!
¡Elegid las palabras!
¿Sobre qué tema?
¡Lo que queremos!*

*Sobre la música,
Sobre el grupo.
¡Las palabras fantásticas!
¡Buena suerte! ¡Buena suerte!*

Translation
So today, we're doing a rap.
It's very easy, we're doing a rap!

In the first place, there are the words.
In the second place there is the beat.

One, two, three, four make the beat.
Are you going to change it?
No, it's good!

Write! Write! Choose the words.
On what subject? Whatever we want!

About music, about the group.
Fantastic words! Good luck! Good luck!

More ideas for...

Work at school

- Make links between Spanish lessons and music lessons by choosing further examples of music for the children to listen to. Encourage careful listening and attention to detail as they decide which Spanish music style label applies.

- Play the children a short piece of music every day. Let them listen to a short partner conversation between you and your Teaching Assistant about it. (You could prepare and record this in advance.) Then ask the children to hold similar partner or small group conversations about the music. Extend vocabulary by sometimes including a new target phrase or word of the day: for example, *Prefiero;*
  ¡Es fantástico/a!
  ¡Es Malísimo/a!
  ¡Es horrible!
  ¡Es aburrido/a!

- Play **Going shopping!** Give partners the roles of a music shop retailer and a customer who comes in hoping to buy a CD. Provide these words as the framework starter, giving the children their conversation part on a small cue card. Can the partners continue the conversation? Will the customer leave with or without a CD?

  Customer: Buenos días.
  Shop assistant: Buenos días.
  Customer: Quiero un CD.
  Shop assistant: Te gusta la música folclórica?
  Customer: Si, pero prefiero la música...

Work at home

- Give the children photocopiable 14B to take home and perform for a family audience. Suggest they ask family members to help them compose an additional verse or a new short rap about the family. At school, make a grand display of the work under the title *¡Es el rap!*

- Ask the children to research current pop stars in Spain. Are Spanish singers popular in this country as well? Do they always sing in Spanish? Have the children heard of any English pop stars who have recorded songs in Spanish? Suggest the children ask their family what they have heard. The children could present their findings in the format of a pop music magazine.

- Give the children a copy of this shop conversation in a play. Explain that the characters are saying their own words, but not in the correct places! Can the children write the conversation in the correct order?

  Customer: Buenos días.
  Shop assistant: Adiós.
  Customer: ¡No, no me gusta la música jazz!
  Customer: Voy a comprar un CD.
  Shop assistant: ¿Te gusta la música jazz?
  Customer: Gracias.
  Shop assistant: ¿Te gusta la música folclórica?
  Customer: Adiós
  Shop assistant: Buenos días.
  Shop assistant: Hay un buen CD de la música pop.
  Customer: Si, pero prefiero la música pop.

- Remind the children about their music group from Lessons 3 and 4. Suggest their group needs publicity. Suggest making an advertising poster with pictures of them, their instruments, and certainly the group's name.

There are many world famous Spanish musician and composers. Plácido Domingo and José Carreras are wonderful opera singers. Manuel de Falla composes popular folk music.

Unit 15 – Vamos al colegio

(On the way to school)

Unit theme
Getting to school

Teaching points
- Describing a journey to school
- Local places
- Simple directions
- Telling the time on the half-hour
- The alphabet

Grammar
- Using *hay*
- Using adverbial time phrases

Language sounds
Matching letter strings to sounds.

Vocabulary

Cuando voy al colegio…	When I go to school…
Paso…	I pass…
Llego a…	I arrive at
por delante de	in front of
cinco minutos más tarde	five minutes later
por fin	finally
Giro	I turn
a la derecha	(to/on the) right
a la izquierda	(to/on the) left
todo recto	straight ahead
No entiendo	I don't understand
Repite, por favor	Repeat, please
una tienda	a shop
una cafetería	a café
un museo	a museum
una oficina de correos	a post office
un río	a river
una estación (de tren)	a (train) station
un banco	a bank
una iglesia	a church

Additional vocabulary for teachers

El número…	Number…
¿Qué letra es?	Which letter is it?
la casilla	the square (in a grid)
Cruzo	I cross
después	after that
entonces	next
el paso de peatones	the pedestrian crossing

Lesson 1 ¿Qué letra es? (Which letter is it?)

Resources:
One copy of photocopiable 15A; a beanbag or soft ball

- Write the thirty letters of the Spanish alphabet on the whiteboard and, using photocopiable 15A, part 1 as your pronunciation guide, say the letters in Spanish, the children repeating them after you.

- Arrange the whiteboard letters into the **Alphabet rap!** shown on the photocopiable. Sing the rap with the children, emphasising rhymes.

- Divide the class into groups, assigning each a section of the **Alphabet rap!** When possible, match the number of letters and group members, but some children may have to share a letter.

- Let group members work out who will sing or chant what. Will they have individual singers or chant letters together?

- Hold a class performance of the **Alphabet rap!** every group singing on cue.

- Check attendance figures by playing **Number ping-pong**. With everyone standing, point to someone to start counting: they say *uno* and point to someone to carry on. After saying a number and 'batting' it to a successor, children sit down. Play again, starting with someone else to make sure your attendance record is accurate.

- Progress to counting in tens from 10 to 100. (See Units 2, 8 and 9 in Book 1) with a game of **Beanbag challenge**. Form a class circle, you in the centre with a bean bag. Toss the bag to someone, at the same time calling out a multiple of 10: they throw it back to you, saying the next multiple of 10 or they are out.

- Return to the letters on the whiteboard and assign each, in alphabetical order, a number between 1 and 30.

- Combine numbers and letters oral work by asking, for example, *¿El número 15, qué letra es?* In response, the children write on their individual whiteboards and say the letter *m*.

Follow-up
Put the children into pairs to play **Combination code**. Using photocopiable 15A, part 2, read aloud sets of number words, the children writing them as numerals. Ask them to hold up their answers before you reveal the correct numerals. Leave these combinations on display for **Codebreakers**, the children using the alphabet-number code to decipher the secret words. Challenge the children to make encrypted secret words or a short message to try on a partner. Will anyone vary the alphabet-number code? (For example, change the direction of the numbering).

Lesson 2 ¿Sí o no? (Yes or no?)

Resources:
Symbols to represent places; a pointing arrow; paper with large squares

- Display an empty grid of 7x7 large squares. (You could create this on an interactive whiteboard.)

- Label the horizontal axis of the grid with the letters **A-F**; label the vertical axis with the numbers **1-7**.

- Put your pointer on a square and ask for its coordinates, its horizontal axis first. Demonstrate saying and writing an answer, for example *la casilla B, 2*. Get everyone talking by encouraging partners to tell each other their answer before you accept answers.

- Progress to naming coordinates, the children working out which square you are referring to and where the pointer should go.

- Explain that this grid is to help you plan and locate places in a town centre.

- Display map symbols for your places, naming the places for the children to repeat: *una tienda, una cafetería, un museo, una oficina de correos, una iglesia, una estación, un río*. Make the vocabulary familiar by playing **Read my lips** in which you mouth the word and the children say it aloud.

- Place symbols on your grid and make statements: for example, *Hay una cafetería en la casilla C, 3*. Each time, the children must confirm or reject your statement with *sí* or *no*.

- Progress to longer answers: *Sí, hay una cafetería* or *No, lo siento* (No, I'm sorry). If the grid is an interactive whiteboard, conceal places with a special screen. When children answer, erase the screen and reveal what is there.

- Make regular changes to places and grid locations, and let children take your role.

Follow-up
Ask the children to make a similar grid and place symbols for their town layout. Underneath their grid they should write some mixed true and false *Hay ...* statements about places and their coordinates. Will a partner spot which to confirm, which to reject?

Lesson 3 Vamos al colegio (On the way to school)

Resources:
Six large cards and six small cards with place names from Lesson 2; a prepared route for a journey to school passing known places; prepared journey descriptions

- Revise the place names from Lesson 2 with these games:

- ○ **Read my lips**: mouth the word for the children to say aloud.

- ○ **Show me**: Put the children into groups, each child drawing one place symbol. Say a place name. Does the correct group member stand up?

- ○ **Stop the bus!** Hang large, place names at different locations in the room. Explain they are also bus stops in the town. Play music, the children bustling around town. Pause the music for everyone to choose a bus stop to wait at. Holding your small place name cards, instruct someone: *Coge una carta* (Take a card) and read it out. Passengers waiting there are out: this bus does not stop there! Keep re-starting the game, the remaining children choosing a bus stop each time the music pauses and a new card picked. After five journeys, who kept choosing a good stop?

- On the whiteboard, draw a simple map of a journey, place symbols marked. Add a house (*una casa*) to the beginning of the map, a school (*un colegio*) to the end. (Save this map to re-use in Lesson 4).

- Explain that the map shows your journey to school. Indicate relevant parts as you say: *Cuando voy al colegio, paso por delante de una estación. Paso por delante de una cafetería.*

- Introduce time into the description: *Cuando voy al colegio, paso por delante de una estación. Cinco minutos más tarde paso por delante de una cafetería. Por fin, llego al colegio.*

- Re-read your last description for groups to mime actions and locations.

Follow-up
Give the children an enlarged copy of Photocopiable 15B, Part 1 to do. Make a preliminary oral reading of Juan's words with the children and display a dictionary bank of new vocabulary.

Lesson 4 ¿Qué hora es? (What time is it?)

Resources:
The class puppet; map and journey description from Lesson 3; a large teaching clock with movable hands; small teaching clocks (if available) for the children

- Use a teaching clock to revise (from Unit 11, Book 1) time on the hour. Practise the question *¿Qué hora es?* and the answer *Son... las diez.* (It's... 10 o'clock.)

- Bring out Juan, your puppet. Encourage the class to ask him *¿Qué hora es?*

- As Juan alters the hands to half-past 10, let him answer (through you) *Son las diez y media.*

- Repeat Juan's game with other half-past times. Progress to a child re-setting the time (only to a time on the half hour) and the class saying it.

- Write four time statements. Can the children show or draw the clocks? Reverse the activity: draw a clock and let the children write the time statements.

- Play your special version of **What's the time Mr Wolf?** from Unit 11, Lesson 3. With you as lion, the children must listen for half hours as well as hours. (A half hour will need half a pace.) Emphasise that your animal noise (*¡roarr!*) means they must vanish!

- Ask Juan *¿A qué hora vas al colegio?* Answer for him: for example, *Voy al colegio a las siete y media.* Let partners exchange this information saying, to the nearest half hour, when they set off for school.

- Show the children your journey map from Lesson 3. Add a clock and a sentence to your house symbol. For example: *Voy al colegio a ...las siete.* Similarly, add a clock and sentence to your school symbol. For example: *Llego al colegio a... las siete y media.* Can the children suggest other points on your map for a clock face and time statement?

- Use Photocopiable 15B, Part 2 for the children to make a simple map of their journey to school, places marked with symbols, and important time(s) marked with clock faces. (Emphasise keeping to the nearest half hour).

Follow-up
Ask the children to write a short piece of text to explain their journey. Put useful vocabulary on display. Let the children make a presentation of their audio visual material to the class; less confident children may prefer to present their work to a partner or small group.

Alphabet rap!

a (ah) b (beh)	c (seh) ch (cheh) d (deh)	e (eh) f (efeh) g (heh)	h (ah cheh) i (ee)	j (hota)
k (kah) l (eleh) ll (ejeh)	m (eme) n (ene) ño (enyeh)	o (oh) p (peh)	q (cu)	r (ereh) rr (erreh)
s (eseh) t (teh)	u (oo) v (veh)	w (doble veh)	x (ekees) y (ee griega)	z (zeta)

Combination codes

Number groups:

tres, diez, dieciséis, tres, dieciocho

nueve, uno, veintinueve

quince, veinticinco, veintitrés, seis, dieciocho

dos, uno, dieciséis, tres, dieciocho

tres, uno, veintitrés, uno

Codebreakers

Combination codes

3, 10, 16, 3, 18

9, 1, 29

15, 25, 23, 6, 18

2, 1, 16, 3, 18

3, 1, 23, 1

<u>Secret words:</u> ***cinco, hay, museo, banco, casa***

Voy al colegio

Read Juan's description of his journey from home to school.
Write in his missing time phrases.
Draw a map to help others follow his route.

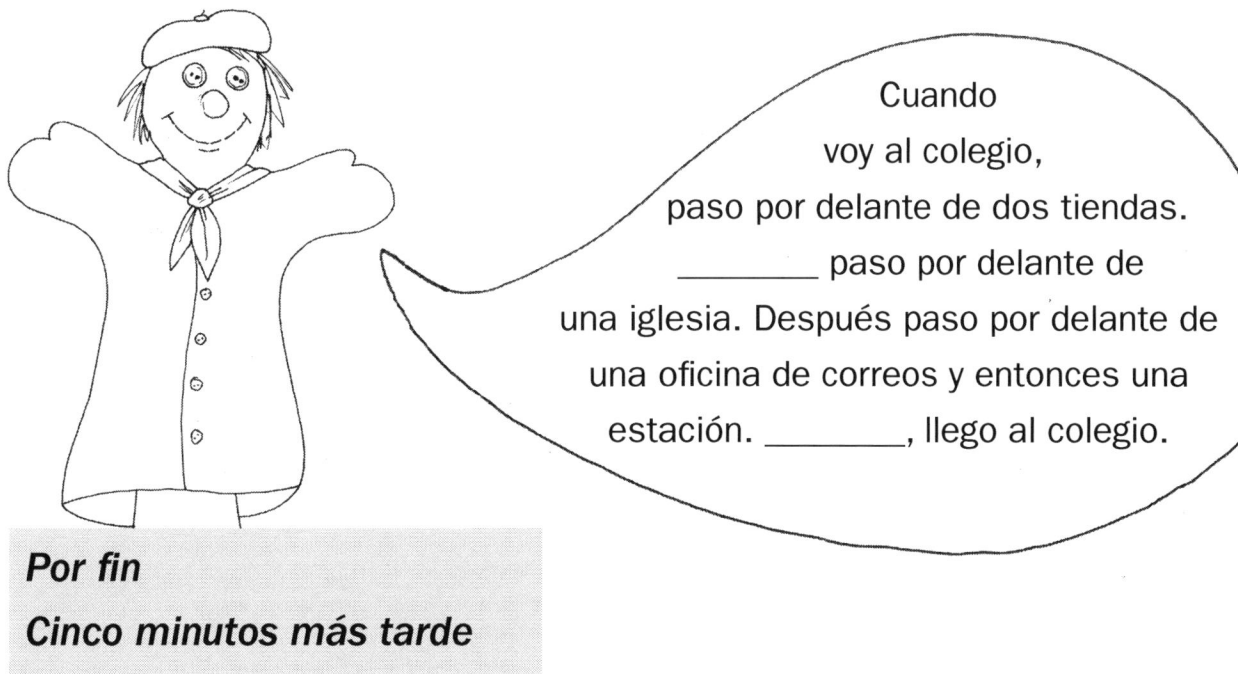

Cuando voy al colegio, paso por delante de dos tiendas. _____ paso por delante de una iglesia. Después paso por delante de una oficina de correos y entonces una estación. _____, llego al colegio.

Por fin
Cinco minutos más tarde

Draw a map of your journey from home to school.
Write a description of the journey.
Include at least one time and one time phrase.

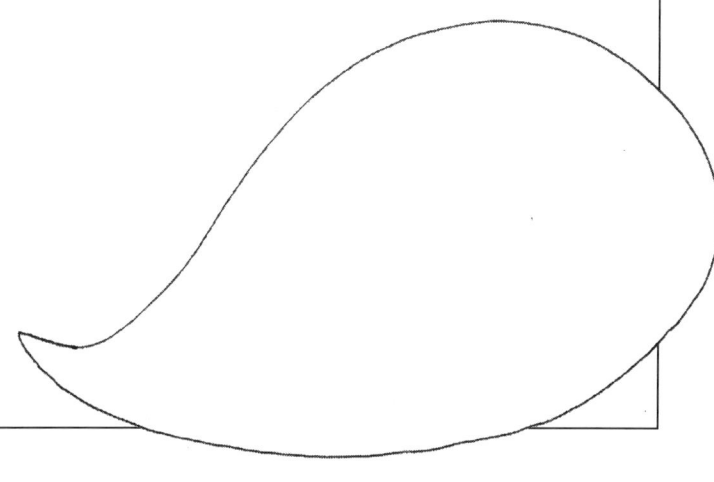

More ideas for…

Work at school

- Make **Alphabet rap!** a class favourite by holding regular performances. Incorporate audio and visual elements so the children say and see letters. Learning and remembering the alphabet will become easy and fun. Practise the alphabet with children spelling out a famous person's initials or full name. Can others work out the identity?

- Extend your work on school journeys to include mode of travel. Revise the relevant vocabulary from Unit 7, Book 1 and the question ¿Cómo vas al colegio? and answers such as Voy al colegio a pie. Suggest the children add this information to their writing from Lesson 4's **Follow-up**.

- Teach the children these directions: *a la derecha; a la izquierda; todo recto*. Provide plenty of space in a game of **Follow your nose**: you call out a series of directions, using imperatives; the children have to finish up facing the correct way. Directions could include: *Girad … a la izquierda* (Turn … left). *Ir…. todo recto* (Go … straight on). Make the game more fun by creating 'places' in the room: for example, *una cafetería*. Play the game again. Will your directions take them to the right place? Challenge the children to direct a partner to a place. Add new vocabulary: *el paseo de peatones* and *cruza* (cross).

- Improve the children's speaking, listening and spelling by displaying a short account of your journey. Omit letter strings from some words. Read the account aloud saying the words in full, as if the letters were there.

Work at home

- Create a worksheet of shopping bags, each containing a muddled version of one of these sentences:

  Voy al colegio a las ocho.
  Voy al colegio a pie.
  Hay una cafetería en el camino al colegio.
  Paso por delante de una oficina de correos.
  Hay un paseo de peatones.
  Cruzo la calle al paseo de peatones.
  Por fin llego al colegio.
  Llego al colegio a las ocho y media.

- Give each child a copy of the worksheet. Ask them to cut out each shopping bag, take out and sort the bag's words and write them as a sentence. Challenge them to prove their understanding by adding illustrations.

- Ask the children to draw a simple map of a journey they make from home to a local shop. Give them a vocabulary list so they can write a description of their journey - the places they pass and the directions they follow. Include sentence-starters and helpful phrases in the vocabulary list. For example:

  Cuando voy a la tienda …; paso por delante de …; …; giro…; cruzo….

- Give the children a page of clock faces and a list of time sentences. Can the children match each clock to its time sentence?

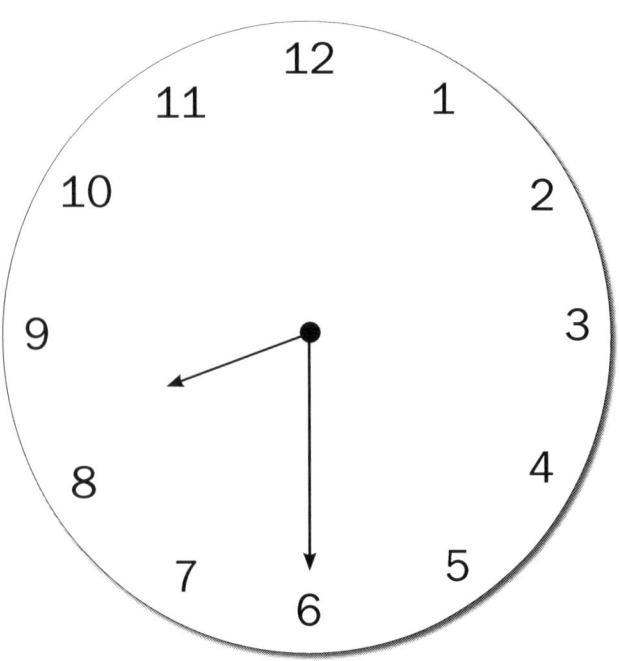

In Spain the school day starts at 8.30am and finishes at 4.30pm. At secondary school the day is longer: it starts at 8.00am and finishes at 5.00pm.

Unit 16 – Una escena de la playa

(Beach scene)

Unit theme
Looking at a painting (of a beach)

Teaching points
- Describing a scene or place
- Using adjectives to add interest and detail
- Writing instructions

Grammar
- *Dormir* (irregular third person singular, present tense: *él/ella duerme*)
- Imperatives: *tú* form
- *Es, no es* + noun

Language sounds
- *z* and *c* (*ce, ci*)
- *gu* (before *i* and *e*)
- *qui* (as in *tranquilo*)

Vocabulary

La niña duerme	The little girl is sleeping
El barco navega	The boat glides along
El niño nada	The little boy is swimming
Las mujeres/señoras pasean / hablan/juegan/miran al mar	The women/ladies walk/talk/play/look at the sea
Es...	It is...
No es...	It is not...

(Instructions are given in the familiar/singular form)

Coge	Take
Déjalo	Leave
Pon	Place/put
Mezcla	Mix
Decora	Decorate
la arena	the sand
el cielo	the sky
el barco	the boat
la playa	the beach
una bahía	a bay
un acantilado	a cliff
una cueva	a cave
las conchas (f)	shells
las rocas (f)	rocks
los guijarros (m)	pebbles
una cesta	a basket

Additional vocabulary for teachers

Me gusta mucho	I really like
Vamos a jugar a Tres en raya	We're going to play **Noughts and Crosses**
¿Qué hace el barco/la niña/la señora?	What is the boat/little girl/lady doing?
¿Qué hacen las personas/ señoras?	What are the people/ladies doing?

Resources
A photocopy of a painting of a beach scene for example, *Pescadoras valencianas* (Valencian fisherwomen) by Sorolla

Lesson 1 Una escena de la playa (Beach scene)

Resources:
A coloured copy of a beach scene (preferably *Pescadoras valencianas* by Sorolla); large PE hoops in assorted colours; coloured PE bands

- Put a mixture of red, blue, yellow and green large PE hoops on the floor.

- Revising colour vocabulary from Unit 4, Book 1 call out a colour, for example *rojo*. Watch to see who moves next to or into a red hoop.

- Change the hoops to piles of PE bands. Call out a colour, for example *amarillo*: if children go and put on a yellow band, they are in the correct team!

- On the whiteboard, create a colour chart: black, white, brown, purple, orange and pink.

- Put the children into pairs. Choosing a pair, give the instruction, for example, *Tocad rosa*. If they touch pink, they win a point.

- Display a coloured copy of a beach scene painting, preferably *Pescadoras valencianas* (Valencian fisherwomen) by Sorolla.

- Identify about eight relevant, important nouns in the painting: for example *la arena, el cielo, el barco,* and *el mar*. Write the words and let the children practise saying them.

- Play class **Pictogram**, in which you say a descriptive colour sentence about an item in the painting: for example, *El mar es verde* (The sea is green). Challenge the children to draw and colour quickly what you describe.

- Put the children into pairs or small groups for small games of **Pictogram**, individuals or pairs writing a secret, descriptive colour sentence about the painting, and taking turns reading it to the rest of the group. Will the others draw and colour what the writer meant?

Follow-up
Suggest the children make a list (in English) of 10 nouns represented in the painting that they do not know the Spanish words for. Give them bilingual dictionaries so they can write the Spanish equivalents.

Lesson 2 ¿Qué hace la niña? (What is the little girl doing?)

Resources:
Two cardboard dice: one dice with a colour word written on each face, the other with a noun from Lesson 1 on each face;

- Revise the noun and colour vocabulary from Lesson 1 with this game:

  ○ Have two large dice: one with a colour word on each face; the other with one of the nouns from Lesson 1 on each face.

  ○ Put the children into pairs. Roll both dice and choose two children to work together to put the words showing into a sentence. Does the class know what the children say?

- Display the Sorolla painting again and introduce some relevant verbs. For example, say *La niña duerme.* Then ask the question *¿Qué hace la niña?* (What is the little girl doing?) so the children repeat the answer *La niña duerme*. Do this with other questions and answers: (*¿Qué hace el barco?*) *El barco navega;* (*¿Qué hace la mujer?*) *La mujer mira el mar.*

- Use the plural question form, asking *¿Qué hacen los niños?* (What are the children doing?) Answer with *Los niños nadan.* (The children are swimming.) *¿Qué hacen las mujeres?* (What are the women doing?) Answer with *Las mujeres hablan.* (The women are talking.)

- Make the children familiar with the verbs' meanings by playing these games:

  ○ Call out one of the sentences for the class to mime.

  ○ Individuals act as caller, saying one of the sentences for the class to mime.

  ○ Divide the class into five groups. Give each group a role in the picture: *el niño, la niña, la mujer, el barco, las mujeres*. Ask the groups to freeze-frame their part. Write their five answer sentences on the whiteboard. In turn, bring groups to life to say their sentence.

- Read aloud this new word scene so everyone can act what is happening now.

La niña mira al mar,
El niño juega.
La mujer duerme.
El barco navega.
Las mujeres pasean.

Follow-up
Write the above description on the whiteboard. Write a box of nouns and verbs at the side. Ask the children to create and write their own new beach scene and draw the beach scene to fit their writing.

Lesson 3 La playa (The beach)

Resources:
The copy of the painting being studied; individual copies of Photocopiable 16A; UK tourist board websites with images of popular UK beaches

- Display the Sorolla painting and these sentences: *Hay una cesta. La niña mira al mar. El pequeño barco navega.*

- Ask partners to work on one sentence at a time, adding a colour description to each sentence. Choose an answer and amend your written sentence accordingly: for example, *Hay una cesta amarilla. La niña mira al mar verde. El pequeño barco rojo navega.*

- Highlight the colour descriptions. Ask: *What type of words are they?* (Adjectives) *Can you identify an adjective already in one sentence?* (*pequeño*)

- Point out the position of the colour adjectives: most of them follow the nouns they describe. Explain that this is the adjective's usual position in Spanish, but there are many exceptions (such as *pequeño* and *grande*) that may precede the noun.

- Ask: *What happens to an adjective's spelling?* Emphasise its agreement with its noun: *amarilla, rojo.*

- Give the children further oral practice by creating sentences about the painting, the children adding adjectives. Demonstrate the adjectives' spelling.

- Examine the physical details of the painting's beach and setting. Ask: *Are there resemblances to seaside places you know in the UK and Spanish-speaking countries?*

- Use Internet tourist board sites to show images of well-known English beaches: for example, Bournemouth, Brighton and Torquay. Consider typical physical characteristics, finding opportunities to introduce these words: *un acantilado* (a cliff); *una bahía* (a bay); *una cueva* (a cave); *las conchas* (shells); *las rocas* (rocks); *los guijarros* (pebbles). List and say the words for the children to repeat after you.

- Display an enlarged picture of one popular English beach. Ask the children questions to elicit affirmative answers: for example, *¿Es una bahía? Sí, es una bahía. ¿Hay las conchas? Sí, hay las conchas.* Elicit a negative response: for example, *¿Hay la arena? No, hay los guijarros.*

- Finish by displaying and reading aloud the poem on the top section of Photocopiable 16A. Create a glossary, next to the poem, with the meanings of some unfamiliar words. Explain the construction *tan... como* (as... as).

Follow-up
Give the children a copy of Photocopiable 16A to follow the words as you read the poem aloud again, encouraging them to join in. Leave the glossary on display as partners do the work on the photocopiable.

Lesson 4 ¡Mezcla una playa! (Mix a beach!)

Resources:
One copy of Photocopiable 16A; individual copies of Photocopiable 16B

- Display and read aloud the poem *La playa* from Photocopiable 16A.

- Let the children use their answers to the questions on the bottom half of the photocopiable as you discuss the poem and its meaning:

> The Beach
> The blue sky is as calm sea as the sea. The calm sea is as large as the sand. The large sand is as golden as the sun. The golden sun is as gleaming as the shells. The gleaming shells are as white as the clouds. The white clouds are as silent as the boats. The silent boats are as blue as the sky. How lovely is the beach!

- Highlight changes in adjectives' spelling (for example, *dorada* to *dorado*; *azul* to *azules*) to accommodate noun changes: feminine to masculine, singular to plural.

- Point out similes in the poem and the Spanish construction *tan...como...* (as... as ...).

- Write, say and explain these imperative verbs: *pon; añade; mezcla; decora; deja.*

- Agree on actions as you test the children's memories in these games:

  ○ **Cook together** Call out an imperative for everyone to obey. Have quick changes of action. Do some chefs go wrong?

- ○ **Do your bit** Put the children into five groups, numbering each group. Call out a group's number and imperative. When every group is performing, check to see who is messing up the recipe by not following their instruction.

- ○ **Watch my lips** Keep the children in five groups. Visit each group in turn, silently mouthing an imperative. Does every group do the correct action?

- Suggest using these imperatives to start lines in a class poem about a beach. (You could use the Sorolla painting, a postcard scene, an imaginary beach.)

- Work together to construct and write simple lines. Give time for partner or small group discussion before you ask for and accept ideas. Encourage the addition of adjectives and detail. Talk about an ending. Will you name your beach? For example:

> *Pon el mar tranquilo*
> *Y un cielo azul.*
> *Añade la arena amarilla*
> *Y un barco rojo.*
> *Mezcla con los niños que nadan.*
> *Decora con los guijarros blancos.*
> *Déjalo al sol brillante.*
> *Es la playa de Bournemouth!*

- Read the poem together. Do the children have a mental picture of the beach?

Follow-up
Give the children Photocopiable 16B to use the same recipe format to write their own beach poem. Suggest working in pairs, doing initial drafts and using the class poem for guidance.

Madrid is located about 350 km from the coast, but in 2008 the Madrid Urban beach was created in the middle of the city. This allows Madrid's tourists and locals to enjoy a seaside atmosphere without travelling.

La playa

El cielo azul es tan tranquilo como el mar.
El mar tranquilo es tan grande como la arena.
La arena grande es tan dorada como el sol.
El sol dorado es tan brillante como las conchas.
Las conchas brillantes son tan blancas como las nubes.
Las nubes blancas son tan silenciosas como los barcos.
Los barcos silenciosos son tan azules como el cielo.
¡Qué bonita es la playa!

Read the poem with your partner. Discuss each question before you write an answer.

What is the poem about?

Find three reasons why the poet likes the beach.

Which Spanish colour adjective describes the boat?

What two items are described as blancas?

List six other adjectives in the poem.

What is the sand compared to?

Why does the poet make this comparison?

¡Uno, dos, tres!

Mezcla una playa…

Añade … _____
_____

Mezcla … _____
_____

Decora … _____
_____

Déjalo … _____
_____
_____

More ideas for…

Work at school

- In a dance lesson, put the children into small groups to plan and perform a sequence of movements that bring the Sorolla painting to life.

- Give the children the top half of photocopiable 16A. Ask them to underline or circle, in different colours, the words containing:

    gu (before *i* or *e*);
    qui

Let the children listen as you say the words. Can they hear the differences in the sounds? Working on one sound at a time, agree on an action (such as thumb up or thumb down) for children to use when they hear that sound in an assortment of words you read aloud. Award 'Great listener!' badges.

- Hold a poetry festival in which everyone takes the role of both performer and audience: partners read aloud their poems from the **Follow-up** to Lesson 4 to a group or the whole class. Encourage the audience to listen carefully for the colours being painted by the poems.

- Suggest that the children do a painting or postcard to illustrate their 'beach recipe' poem, written in the **Follow-up** to Lesson 4. Create a display of the pictures and words.

Work at home

- Ask the children to see what they can find out, using books or the Internet about Sorolla and his beach paintings. Is there a similar painting by another artist? Suggest they use an art book as they find three other beach paintings they find appealing, and list their titles and artists.

- Ask the children to bring from home a favourite photograph they, or a family member, has taken of a beach they like in the UK or a Spanish-speaking country. Invite the children to show and talk about this beach to a partner or group, explaining what they like.

- Provide the children with a vocabulary sheet so that they can compose a short paragraph in Spanish about one of their favourite beaches (perhaps the beach in the photograph in the previous activity.) Provide helpful sentences starters they may choose to use:

  ○ **Es la playa de…** (for example, **Blackpool**)

  ○ **La arena es…**

  ○ **Hay…**

  ○ **Me gusta mucho…**

The Costa del Sol, with wonderful sunny beaches on its 160km of coastline, is a favourite holiday destination for Spanish people and visitors.

Unit 17 – Los cuatro estaciones

(The four seasons)

Unit theme
Responding to a poem
Responding to a piece of classical music

Teaching points
- Making simple statements (about seasons)
- Describing the weather (present and past)
- Using adjectives as antonyms

Grammar
- Preposition: *en* (with the seasons)
- Adjectives: position and agreement
- Imperfect verb tense (For example, *Hacía sol/viento*)

Language sounds
- Matching sounds to writing

Vocabulary

la primavera	spring
el verano	summer
el otoño	autumn
el invierno	winter
en primavera/verano/ otoño/ invierno	in spring/summer/ autumn/ winter
Hacía buen/mal tiempo	The weather was good/bad
luminoso	light
oscuro	dark
contento	happy
triste	sad
caliente	hot
alegre	happy
visité	I visited
cálido	warm
lleno de color	colourful
sombrío	dull
agitado	excited
tranquilo	calm
gracioso	funny
serio	serious
Ven/Quédate conmigo	Come to/Stay (singular) with me
Los colores son …	The colours are …
Aplaude	Clap (singular) your hands
Golpea con el pie	Tap (singular) your feet
el prado	the meadow
la rama	the branch
el almendro	the almond tree
un grillo	a cricket
las abejas	bees
las amapolas	poppies
los lirios	lilies
las campanillas	bluebells
una margarita	a daisy

Additional vocabulary for teachers

el verano pasado/que viene	last/next summer
el año pasado/que viene	last/next year
la semana pasada/que viene	last/next week
ayer	yesterday
hoy	today
mañana	tomorrow
¿Qué estación es?	Which season is it?
Emparejad/empareja un color con una estación	Match (plural/singular) a colour to a season
Describid/Describe una estación	Describe (plural/singular) a season
Borra la pizarra	Wipe the board
¿De qué color es?	What colour is it?

Resources
A recording of Vivaldi's 'The Four Seasons'; the class puppet

Lesson 1 ¿Qué estación es? (Which season is it?)

Resources:
Class puppet; calendar pictures representative of the time of year

- Revise the months of the year (See Unit 3, Book 1) by chanting them, in these groups, to a simple tune:

- *Enero, febrero; marzo, abril, mayo; junio, julio, agosto; septiembre, octubre, noviembre; diciembre.* Encourage the children to join in as you repeat the song.

- Ask the children to write their birthday month on their individual whiteboard. Sing the song again, this time children standing, holding up their whiteboard and singing alone when their month is reached.

- Announce that you are dividing the classroom into seasons. Hang signs in four different areas of the room: *el invierno; la primavera; el verano; el otoño.*

- Go to each sign in turn, hold up a representative picture (for example a snowy field) and announce, for example, *el invierno*, the children repeating the season after you.

- Display outdoor scenes where the weather and stage of plant or animal life are obvious. Ask *¿Qué estación es?* the children replying *Es ... el invierno.*

- Make statements about months and the season they are in: for example, *Febrero es en invierno; abril es en primavera.*

- Make sure that you use example sentences that use *en invierno, en primavera, en verano, en otoño.* Point out the use of *en* to express in a season. Let the children repeat the four phrases after you.

- Tell the children which season your birthday is in: *Mi cumpleaños es en invierno.* Bring out Juan, your class puppet, to tell the children (via your disguised voice) his birthday season.

- Invite the children to tell a talk partner their birthday season. (Their whiteboard month label will let them help each other.)

- Ask the children to sit in the appropriate area of the room, taking their whiteboard labels with them as identification. Suggest checks: 'Are others in my month here? Which other months are in this area?'

- Play a game in which you hold up assorted calendar pictures. The correct season has only one minute to make its claim: *Es...el verano.* If correct, they win the picture. Which season successfully claims most?

Follow-up
Suggest having a living interactive calendar of the four seasons. Challenge the groups to plan and practise a tableau, that will come to life and and make its statement (*Es...el verano.*) when you point the remote control at them. Hold a class performance of the cycle of the year's seasons.

Lesson 2 El verano pasado... (Last summer...)

- Revise some weather phrases from Units 7 and 12, Book 1 that use *hacer*: *Hace buen tiempo* (It is good weather) *Hace calor* (It is hot) *Hace frío* (It is cold). Explain that they are all in the present tense. Do the children know how to tell? (The verbs)

- Display a postcard - perhaps of the Royal Palace in Madrid. Write on the whiteboard: *El verano pasado, visité Madrid. Hacía calor.*

- Read the text aloud. Let the children, in pairs, try to work out the meaning. Can they tell if the text is about the present, past or future? What clues can they find?

- Share thoughts and highlight the time clue *pasado* and the past tense verbs: *visité* and *Hacía calor.* Agree on the text's meaning. (Last summer, I visited Madrid. It was hot.)

- Explain that *hacía* is the imperfect tense of the verb *hacer*; the imperfect tense is used to describe weather in the past.

- Teach the children other weather phrases that use *hacer* in the imperfect tense: *Hacía mal tiempo/ buen tiempo/frío/viento/sol.* Use weather symbols as the children practise the phrases.

- Play a game with this equipment:

  ○ two small soft balls: a red one labelled 'present'; a blue one labelled 'past';

  ○ a pack of weather symbol cards. (Make sure they are types of weather that use *hacer* in their weather phrase.)

- Put the children into pairs; throw one of them a ball; invite their partner to pick a (face down) weather card. Can the partners make a suitable weather phrase with the appropriate tense of *hacer*? Give every pair a turn. How many pairs win a point?

Follow-up
Give the children photocopiable 17A to create and write sentences about last summer's holiday in Spain. Suggest the children work in pairs.

Lesson 3 El verano ha venido (Summer has come)

Resources:
Photocopiable 17B; an interactive whiteboard, if available

- Give the instructions *Aplaude* (Clap your hands) and *Golpea con el pie* (Tap your feet) demonstrating what they mean. Play **Which is which?** as you give sudden instructions, the children deciding quickly which action is needed.

- Read aloud the chorus of the Spanish poem on photocopiable 17B, the children doing their actions. Did they hear which season was mentioned? (Summer)

- Display the whole poem and read it aloud, the children joining in and acting the chorus. Give time for partner discussion as you ask: What is the poem about? What things change in each verse? (The animal and the place)

- Remove the poem from display and write these lines, in their muddled order, on the whiteboard. (Have the text ready on your interactive whiteboard.)

    ¡Ven, ven, ven!
    ¡Aplaude! ¡Aplaude!
    Una abeja me dijo "Ven,
    En el campo, esta mañana
    Es el verano que vuelve.
    El verano está en camino."

- Colour code the lines by putting a different circle of colour next to each.

- Give the children, individually or in pairs, six separated, interlocking bricks of the equivalent colours.

- As you read the lines of the poem aloud in the correct order (from your copy of photocopiable 17B) the children must identify the line and its colour. Their aim is to finish with their bricks in the correct colour order. Read the lines more than once.

- Order the lines on the whiteboard as the children display their results. Were some lines easy to place? Which spoken words were easiest to match to their written forms?

Follow-up
Give the children the top half of photocopiable 17B. Ask them to underline the animal and its habitat in each verse. Suggest they make a glossary, listing these six nouns and their written and pictorial meanings. Give partners access to a bilingual dictionary as they work on adding an animal and place to the poem as they write an additional verse. (Animals could include: *una mariquita* (a ladybird), *una avispa* (a wasp), *una golondrina* (a swallow). Habitats could include: *el prado* (the meadow), *el macizo* (the flower bed), *la granja* (the farm)

Lesson 4 La estación preferida (The favourite season)

Resources:
A recording of Vivaldi's 'The Four Seasons'

- Remind the children about the poem on photocopiable 17B about summer's return.

- Suggest that each season is like a person, persuading people that their season is best.

- Write *el invierno; la primavera; el verano; el otoño* on four separate pieces of paper. Agree on and write persuasive words, phrases and lines *el invierno* could say. For example:

  ○ Ven, ven, ven

  ○ El invierno es muy blanco.

  ○ El invierno está en camino."

  ○ Quédate conmigo.

  ○ El invierno es tan fresco.

- Encourage the children to think about weather and colours as you write similar lines, phrases and single words for the other seasons. Suggest adjectives and sentence structures, and show how to adapt ideas and lines from the photocopiable poem.

- Re-form the birthday season groups used in Lesson 1, explaining that each season will try to persuade other people that their season is the best.

- Ask the children to make pairs or groups of three with children in their season and to decide on which persuasive sentence or phrases to say. Encourage originality.

- Give the children time to practise pronunciation, intonation and persuasive facial and body language.

- Ask two seasons – *el invierno* and *el verano* – to form lines facing each other, an alley way between the lines, talk partners standing next to each other.

- Let the children in the other two groups walk down the Persuasion Alley, listening and watching as the children in *el invierno* and *el verano* whisper their lines to them.

- Ask the children in *la primavera* and *el otoño* to vote for which season was more persuasive.

- Change roles: *la primavera* and *el otoño* form lines facing each other, an alley between, and *el invierno* and *el verano* walk between the lines, listening and watching.

- Hold a final contest between the two winners. The class will discover which season they most look forward to returning.

Follow-up
Repeat the Persuasion Alleys, Vivaldi's 'The Four Seasons' playing quietly in the background. Does the same season win?
Give the children written sentences to complete about the season they like:

Prefiero ——— . *Es tan* - Invite them to extend the text. (For example: *Prefiero el verano. Es tan cálido. El verano está lleno de color. Hay un montón de flores.*)

Spain is usually the host for one section of the summer cycle race, the Tour de France.

El verano pasado

Make up six pairs of sentences about your imaginary trip around Spain last year. Each pair of sentences must say where you visited and what the weather was like.

Use this example to help you:
El verano pasado, visité Sevilla. Hacía calor.

El verano pasado	Sevilla	Hacía calor
visité	Barcelona	Hacía frio
	Málaga	Hacía mucho calor
	Granada	Hacía viento
	Alicante	Hacía mal tiempo
	San Sebastián	Hacía sol
		Hacía buen tiempo

El regreso del verano

*En el jardín, esta mañana
Una mariposa me dijo "Ven,
Ven, ven, ven,
El verano está en camino."*

*Coro
¡Aplaude! ¡Aplaude!
Es el verano que regresa.
¡Golpea con el pie!
El verano comienza de nuevo.*

*En el campo, esta mañana
Una abeja me dijo "Ven,
Ven, ven, ven,
El verano está en camino."*

(Coro)

*Cerca del río, esta mañana
Une rana me dijo "Ven,
Ven, ven, ven,
El verano está en camino."*

Translation:

The return of summer
In the garden this morning
A butterfly said to me, "Come,
Come, come, come,
Summer is on its way."

Chorus
Clap your hands! Clap your hands!
Summer is coming again.
Tap your feet!
Summer is starting again.

In the garden this morning
A bee said to me, "Come,
Come, come, come,
Summer is on its way."

(Chorus)

Near the river this morning
A frog said to me, "Come,
Come, come, come,
Summer is on its way.

More ideas for...

Work at school

- Practise the use of *hacer* in the present and past tenses by playing **Today and Yesterday**:

  ○ One child says a weather sentence beginning with *Hoy...*. (For example: *Hoy hace sol.*)

  ○ Their partner replies with an *Ayer ....*sentence. (For example: *Ayer hacía frío.*)

- Expand the children's vocabulary by giving them this written list of adjectives:

  ○ *calido, luminoso, alegre, gracioso, agitado, triste, tranquilo, frío, serio, oscuro,*

  ○ Give the children a bilingual dictionary to find out and write a meaning for each. Ask them to pair the adjectives into antonyms. Can they write any more pairs of antonyms?

- Follow up the last activity in **Work at home**, sharing ideas and working together on a class poem about the return of a different season.

- Use your Persuasion Alley activity from Lesson 4 for a class performance. Put two seasons on either side of the alley and have only a few children (and perhaps yourself) walking through. Include Vivaldi's music, and indicate to the children when they should speak. Encourage clear speech and theatrical movements. Finish by the walkers declaring the class's favourite season: for example: *El otoño es la estación preferida.*

Work at home

- Give the children their list of adjectives and meanings from the second **Work at school** activity. Ask them to use the adjectives in written sentences, being careful about position and agreement. Suggest they try to make up sentences relating to the theme 'Las cuatro estaciones'.

- Invite the children to create an unusual family album, in which they put a picture of each member of their family and pretend that the person is speaking for themselves in a speech bubble and a written sentence stating their birthday season. Supply:

  ○ the sentence beginning: *Mi cumpleaños es ...*

  ○ the preposition and seasons: *en invierno/primavera/verano/otoño.*

- Ask the children to create a pictorial season wheel for the year. In each season, they should write a typical weather and two colours they associate with the season. Supply a vocabulary sheet to help.

- Give the children the Spanish poem on photocopiable 17B. Ask them to plan how and where to change the poem so it is about the return of a different season. What and how many changes will they make?

The climate in many areas of Spain is excellent for winemaking. The Rioja region is particularly famous for the quality of its red wines.

Unit 18 – Los planetas

(The planets)

Unit theme
The planets

Teaching points
- Describing a planet
- Making a statement about a planet's position
- Classifying nouns, adjectives and verbs

Grammar
- Using qualifiers: *bastante, muy, mucho*
- Using prepositions: *cerca de, lejos de*
- Making compound sentences with *porque*

Language sounds
- Phonemes: revising and hearing common phonemes to help writing

Vocabulary

la Tierra	the Earth
la luna	the moon
un nombre	a noun
un nombre propio	a proper noun
un adjetivo	an adjective
porque	because
cerca de (cerca del sol)	near (near the sun)
lejos de (lejos del sol)	far from (far from the sun)
bastante	quite
muy	very
mucho	a lot/very
Hace mucho calor	It is very hot
Hace mucho frío	It is very cold
Mercurio	Mercury
Venus	Venus
Marte	Mars
Júpiter	Jupiter
Saturno	Saturn
Urano	Uranus
Neptuno	Neptune
Plutón	Pluto

Additional vocabulary for teachers

Emparejad/Empareja un día con un planeta	Match (plural/singular) a day with a planet
Subrayad/Subraya	Underline (plural/singular)
Describid/Describe	Describe (plural/singular)
la caja sorpresa	the jack-in-the-box
el siguiente	next
aquí	here
Estoy pensando en …	I'm thinking of …
¿Qué planeta es?	Which planet is it?
¿Por qué?	Why?
porque	because

Resources
Pictures of the planets

Lesson 1 ¿Qué planeta es? (Which planet is it?)

Resources:
Separate pictures of the planets; separate flashcards of each planet's name; copies of photocopiable 18A (enough for one between two children)

- Show a picture of each of the planets in turn, naming them orally: *Mercurio, Venus, la Tierra, Marte, Júpiter, Saturno, Urano, Neptuno, Plutón*. (The internet is a good source of pictures: for example, www.nasa.gov).

- Emphasise pronunciation, the children tapping the number of syllables. Always say the planets in the same order.

- Play **Write what you hear**: you say the name of a planet; the children write the word. Keep the activity fun with partner collaboration. Display a word card answer. Who was correct? Did they hear and spell a phoneme they recognised?

- Give time for pronunciation practice, partners taking turns to be speaker or listener.

- Ask nine children to stand facing the class. Shuffle the word cards and deal a card each, for the nine children to hold their planet name in front of them.

- Put the rest of the class into pairs. Let a pair of children at a time make one position change to the line of nine human planets as the class tries to order them. How many pairs will have to make a change? Play again with new human planets. Does the class order them more quickly.

- Put the children into pairs with one copy of photocopiable 18A, the cards cut out, for these games:

  ○ **Line them up**
    ○ The children spread out their cards, names showing. Can they put the names in order? When they turn the cards over, do the numbers match the positions?

  ○ **What's my name?**
    ○ With the cards in a pile, numbers up, the partners take turns trying to identify the planet belonging to the top card. If correct, that partner wins the card; if wrong, the card is returned, number up, to the bottom of the pile. How many planets do they each win?

- Finish with another game of **Write what you hear**. Have the children got better at recognising oral phonemes and relating them to writing?

Follow-up
Return to the partner game, **What's my name?** Suggest adding to its difficulty: a player only wins the card if they know the name of the planet and can pronounce it to their partner's satisfaction.

Lesson 2 Describid los planetas (Describe the planets)

Resources:
Pictures of the planets, in colour; a soft ball

- Revise the planets' names from Lesson 1. Play **Pass it on**: start a foam ball on a journey around the classroom; whoever catches it says the next planet in the sequence.

- Display pictures of some of the planets, asking the children simple questions about colour or size. For example:

  ○ *Marte es un planeta rojo. ¿Sí o no?*

  ○ *¿Plutón es un planeta grande o pequeño?*

  ○ *¿De qué color es Júpiter?*

  ○ Involve everyone by giving talk partners time to answer each other before you accept an answer from someone.

- Write a description on the whiteboard: *Plutón es un planeta pequeño. Mercurio es un planeta rápido. Marte es un planeta rojo.*

- Ask the children to tell their partner a common noun in the text. Can they identify a proper noun? What adjectives can they point out to their partner?

- Invite some children to underline, in different colours, appropriate words in the whiteboard's text. Let the class read the words aloud.

- Challenge the children to work out an English translation of the text. Does their partner agree?

- Under the Spanish text on the whiteboard, write the English translation. Ask the children's help in underlining the equivalent English common nouns, proper nouns and adjectives as underlined in the Spanish version.

- Invite partners to discuss both texts, particularly the underlined words. Are the words in the two languages similar? What about their sentence positions? Can partners work out and write a rule to help writers who compose a descriptive sentence in Spanish?

- Put the children into groups of six to listen to one another's rules.
- Let the children to write a final version of their rule (and a descriptive sentence demonstrating the rule) for a 'Top writing tips' section on your Spanish notice board.

Follow-up
Ask the children to write a descriptive text of two or three sentences about some planets. Most children should be able to write independently, using a partner as their checker. Less confident children may work in pairs.

Lesson 3 ¿A la derecha o a la izquierda? (To the right or to the left?)

Resources:
Separate flashcards of each planet's name; a flashcard saying *el sol*; sets of flashcards to form sentences (sentences supplied)

- Draw two direction arrows and write underneath: *a la derecha* (right) and *a la izquierda* (left).
- Select nine children to stand in line facing the class. Give them, in muddled order, the nine planet wordcards from Lesson 1.
- Indicate one human planet at a time for the class to call out the direction to move: *a la derecha; a la izquierda;* or *aquí* (here). How long does it take to get the planets in order?
- Give a tenth child the wordcard *el sol*. Where does the class want to position *el sol*? (At the start of the line, next to *Mercurio*.)
- Select five children to stand facing the class and give them, in muddled order, the wordcards for *Plutón es un planeta pequeño*. Let the class call out directions to order the human sentence. Repeat this with the other descriptive sentences used in the text in Lesson 2.
- Put the class into groups of five with wordcards to make a human sentence:
  ○ Hay nueve planetas.
  ○ Hay nueve colores.
  ○ Saturno es un planeta de color naranja.
  ○ Marte es un planeta rojo.
  ○ Júpiter es un planeta pequeño.
  ○ ¿De qué color es Júpiter?

  Can the class read the sentences aloud?

- Introduce and explain *cerca de …* and *lejos de …* Say and write on the whiteboard sentences about children's places in the room. For example: *Sarah está cerca de Laura. Jack está lejos de Laura.* Point out the use of the verbe *estar* (to be) when referring to position. Challenge the children to say a sentence about two classmates.
- Use the qualifiers *bastante* and *muy*: for example, *Jack está bastante cerca de Matthew.* Can the children tell their talk partner a sentence using *bastante*? Explain that *de* changes to *del* if *el* is going to come next: for example *Juan está muy lejos del piano.* (John is very far from the piano.)
- Play **Solar system**, individuals taking the roles of the sun and some planets. (Include Mercury and Pluto.) After the human planets have introduced themselves (*Me llamo … Venus.*) can partners make up a sentence about their positions?

Follow-up
Give the children photocopiable 18B to order the planets and write about their positions.

Lesson 4 El sol y los planetas (The sun and the planets)

Resources:
10 PE hoops; a list of sentences provided; an interactive whiteboard (if possible)

- Divide the class into nine groups, allocating each group a planet.
- Stand in a PE hoop at one end of the room with nine PE hoops at intervals on the floor between you and the other end of the room. Announce: *Me llamo el sol.*
- Invite the groups to place themselves in the correct hoop and announce which planet they are. Is every planet in the correct place?
- Say *El sol hace mucho calor*. Do the children understand? Can they describe their planet's temperature? (Have a word bank on display.) Can they describe their planet's position in relation to you, the sun? (For example: *La Tierra está cerca del sol.*)

- Write this English text on the whiteboard:

    'Mercury is a very hot planet. Mercury is very close to the sun.' Ask the children to think of an English conjunction to join the two simple sentences into one compound sentence. Replace the full stop with 'because'.

- Underneath, write the equivalent, Spanish compound sentence:

    Mercurio es un planeta muy caliente porque Mercurio está muy cerca del sol.

- Ask partners to read the Spanish to each other a few times. Which word would they not have repeated? Agree that the second *Mercurio* is unnecessary. Demonstrate with the new Spanish compound sentence:

- *Mercurio es un planeta muy caliente porque está muy cerca del sol.*

- Point out that there is no need to repeat *Mercurio* in the second half of the sentence.

- Display separate, simple sentences, preferably on an interactive whiteboard. Let the children work with a partner as they decide which to pair into a compound sentence with *porque* or *y*. Where will they omit nouns?

    ○ *La Tierra es bastante caliente. La Tierra está bastante lejos del sol. (porque)*

    ○ *El sol es amarillo. El sol hace mucho calor. (y)*

    ○ *Plutón hace mucho frío. Plutón está muy lejos del sol. (porque)*

Follow-up

Set the children the task of creating a booklet or interactive game. The aim must be to provide information and descriptions of important features of a planet. For example: a game could have multiple choice questions; a board could have lift-up flaps, under which are the answers to questions on the flaps. Let the children consider using computers.

¡Uno, dos, tres!

1	4	7
2	5	8
3	6	9

¡Uno, dos, tres!

Mercurio	Marte	Urano
Venus	Júpiter	Neptuno
la Tierra	Saturno	Plutón

Describid los planetas

Urano
Marte
la Tierra
Mercurio
Júpiter
Neptuno
Saturno
el sol
Plutón
Venus

caliente
muy
bastante
hace
mucho calor
hace mucho frío
cerca de
lejos de

Fill in the missing labels. Check that you have the planets in the correct order.

1. _____ está cerca del sol.
2. _____ est lejos del sol.
3. Mercure _____ muy caliente.
4. Plutón es un planeta _____.
5. Urano _____ está cerca del sol.
6. _____ está lejos del sol.
7. Mercure _____ muy caliente.
8. Plutón es un planeta _____.
9. Urano _____
10. Saturno _____
11. La Tierra _____
12. Saturno _____
13. La Tierra _____

Fill in the missing words in the early sentences. Make up your own descriptions in the later sentences.

More ideas for...

Work at school

- Put the children into twos with 18 blank cards. Ask them to put their cards into pairs: on one card they should write the name of a planet; on the other card, an appropriate description. To play **Pelmanism**, the cards are shuffled and spread out, face down. Partners take turns choosing two to turn over: if a description and planet match, the player keeps the cards; if not, the cards are turned back over, in the same spot. The winner is the player with the most matching pairs at the end of the game.

- Hold a fun games session, in which the children play with other people's packs of cards made in the last activity and the games made in Lesson 4. Reading one another's descriptions and answers will improve the children's Spanish while teaching them about the solar system.

- Throughout the week, give the children regular practice in the use of the qualifiers *bastante* and *muy*: for example, in a science lesson, comment in Spanish as well as English on the temperature of the liquids in the experiment; in a geography lesson, comment in Spanish as well as English on the relative distances between the locations and your school.

Work at home

- After Lesson 1, give the children photocopiable 18A to take home. Suggest they cut out the cards and play regular games of **Line them up** and **What's my name?** so they become familiar with the planets' names and spelling.

- Having introduced the noun *la luna* (the moon) ask the children to find out three simple facts about the moon. Can they use their information to write two or three descriptive sentences in Spanish about the moon?

- Give the children a vocabulary resource of the names of days of the week. Explain that a day of the week is linked to a planet, the sun or the moon. Can the children recognise or discover which day relates to what and why?

Spain has a strong history of astronomical interest. The ROA (The Royal Institute and Observatory of the Spanish Royal Navy) in Cadiz was originally built to teach star navigation to future naval officers. Now it is also responsible for setting Spain's Standard Time.

Unit 19 – Nuestro colegio

(Our school)

Unit theme
School places and routines

Teaching points
- Talking about school routines, subjects and environment
- Reporting breaktime activities, referring to the past
- Telling the time, using half-hours, quarter-hours
- The 24 hour clock notation

Grammar
- Definite and indefinite articles: *el/la; un/una*
- Preterite tense: regular verbs (eg *jugué, hablé*)

Language sounds
- Hard and soft *c*

Vocabulary

¿Qué hora es?	What time is it?
Es mediodía/medianoche	It is midday/midnight
Es la una y media	It is half past one
Son las dos y media	It is half past two
Son las dos y cuarto	It is quarter past two
Son las dos menos cuarto	It is quarter to two
el patio	the playground
el campo de deportes	the playing field
la clase	the classroom
los aseos (m)	the toilets
el recreo	breaktime
Jugué	I played
Hablé	I spoke
Bailé	I danced
Ayudé	I helped
Trabajé	I worked
Canté	I sang
el dibujo	art
el deporte	sport
el español	Spanish
el inglés	English
el francés	French
las matemáticas (f plural)	maths
las ciencias (f plural)	science
la historia	history
la física	physics
la música	music
¡Es la hora!	It's time!
el salón de actos	the hall
el aparcamiento	the car park
la biblioteca	the library
la cocina	the kitchen
la entrada	the entrance
un horario	a timetable
la hora de la comida	lunchtime
ayer	yesterday
¿A qué hora empiezan las clases?	What time does school start?
¿Cuándo es?	When is it?
¿Qué hiciste (durante el recreo)?	What did you do (at breaktime)?
un/una amigo/amiga	a friend
mis amigos/amigas	my friends

Additional vocabulary for teachers

¿Dónde está…?	Where is …?
Cerrad los ojos	Close your eyes
Abrid los ojos	Open your eyes

Resources
Juan, the class puppet

Lesson 1 ¿Qué hora es? (What time is it?)

Resources:
A large teaching clock with movable hands; small teaching clocks for the children to use

- Set a large teaching clock with movable hands to 11 o'clock.

- Write the question ¿Qué hora es? on the whiteboard. Do the children understand? Remind them how to say Son las once. (See Units 11 and 15)

- Repeat the question about new times on the clock, keeping to the hour or half past the hour.

- Introduce mediodía and medianoche, explaining that they both mean 12 o'clock.

- Put the children into twos with small clocks. They must take turns controlling the clock, making a time on the hour or half past the hour. When they show their partner the clock and ask ¿Qué hora es? can their partner say the time and win a point?

- Remind the children how to write a time digitally: for example 11.30. Give them practice after you have said a time sentence: for example, Son las diez y media (10.30).

- Play **Big Ben** by writing in 24 hour digital notation displays on the whiteboard of your clock's future new times (for example, 14.30). For each, ask everyone to secretly set the hands of their individual clock accordingly. Choose two children to set Big Ben. When you all compare results, do most children agree with Big Ben?

- Explain that two buses make journeys between the village centre and school. Ask the children to create an information sheet to send to parents showing:

  ○ the morning departure times of the two buses from the village, and their arrival times at school;

  ○ the afternoon departure times from school of the same two buses, and their arrival times in the village.

- Suggest drawing places and presenting time information in three ways: a clock face; digital recording; a written sentence. Provide an example: a drawn clock face, hands placed appropriately; 16.00; Son las cuatro.

Follow-up
Point out that mediodía and medianoche often cause confusion. Challenge the children, in pairs, to work out a tip to help the class remember which is which. Let them write and illustrate their tip. When you display them, which ones do the class think are good memory prompts?

Lesson 2 Aquí está el colegio (Here is the school)

Resources:
Photographs of important places in the school

- Indicate the classroom and say: Aquí está la clase. Using the same Aquí está… sentence, point out and name these places: el campo de deportes, el patio, los aseos.

- Identify additional places: el aparcamiento, el salón de actos, la biblioteca, la cocina, la entrada.

- Repeat the names as you show the children photographs of the places.

- Turn the pictures over and, in random order, write the names on the whiteboard.

- Set a challenge. Working in pairs, the children must decide which written Spanish name is what place. Encourage deduction, not memory: knowledge of other Spanish vocabulary and similarities between Spanish and English words will help. Provide sentence constructions for Spanish partner discussion: for example, Creo que 'la cocina' es 'the kitchen' en ingles. (I think that 'la cocina' is 'the kitchen' in English.) When checking in a dictionary, one partner can ask for the spelling with ¿Cómo se escribe? (How is that spelt?) The other must reply by spelling out the Spanish letters.

- Share information as a class, the children disclosing how they reached their answers.

- Display the photographs again. Let the class be tour guides: as you point to a picture, they announce it with the sentence Aquí está… (la entrada).

- Put the children into pairs with a copy of photocopiable 19A, the cards and words cut out, for these games:

  ○ **Beat the clock**

    ○ The children spread out their picture cards face up. Having set themselves a time limit, they label the pictures with the words. Do they beat the clock? With the cards placed randomly again, can they beat a new, lower time limit?

  ○ **Pronunciation points**

    ○ The children take turns reading aloud a label. Their partner, acting as judge, holds up a score card of one, two or three. Who wins more pronunciation points?

- ○ **Pelmanism**
  - ○ Picture cards and words are shuffled and spread out face down. Partners take turns revealing two cards. If the cards are a matching picture and label, the player keeps them; if not, they are returned face down to the same places.

Follow-up
Ask the children to draw a map of a tour of the school for prospective pupils and their parents. For each place marked on the map, they should write what they, as tour guide, will say.

Lesson 3 Un horario (A timetable)

Resources:
A large teaching clock with movable hands; small teaching clocks for the children to use

- Use the teaching clock to revise the time work from Lesson 1: set the hands to a time and ask *¿Qué hora es?*

- Set the hands at 11.15 and say *Son las once y cuarto;* set them at 10.45 and say *Son las once menos cuarto.*

- Call out quarter to and quarter past times in Spanish sentences for the children to make on their individual clocks. Invite individuals to be the caller as you watch the children making the time.

- Put on the whiteboard a timetable of a busy day at school, crammed with subjects! Write the subject names in English and use digital time notation beside them.

- Work through the subject names as you, helped by the children and bilingual dictionaries, translate them into Spanish. (Use an interactive whiteboard, with Spanish subject names already concealed by you.)

- Question the children about the timetable: for example, *¿A qué hora es español? (El español es a las dos.)*

- Put the times into 24 hour clock notation and repeat the preceding question for this answer: *El español es a las catorce.*

- Divide the class into two or three teams. Suggest team members put themselves into pairs with *sí* and *no* voting cards. (They could write on individual whiteboards.)

- Invite each team in turn to choose a pair to say a sentence about the time of a subject on the timetable. The rest of the class vote whether the statement is true. After five minutes which team has said more true sentences?

Follow-up
Make a recording and play 'The timetable song' to the children:

Lunes escribo el inglés,
(Monday I write English)

Martes hablo el español,
(Tuesday I speak Spanish)

Miércoles escucho la música,
(Wednesday I listen to music)

Jueves hay la historia,
(Thursday there is history)

¡Viernes es fantástico!
(Friday is fantastic)

¡Me gusta mucho el deporte!
(I really like sport)

Play it a few times, the children listening and beginning to join in. Ask them to list the five days and beside each write that day's subjects(s) in English. When partners compare timetables, have they identified the same subjects? Finally, display the song's words.

Lesson 4 Durante el recreo (At breaktime)

Resources:
Timetable from Lesson 3; class puppet

- Introduce the word *ayer* (yesterday). Display a version of yesterday's timetable, in Spanish. Show times and include breaktime (*el recreo*) and lunchtime (*la hora de la comida*).

- As in Lesson 3, question the children about the times of subjects and breaks. Challenge them to make a statement about the timetable to their talk partner.

- Get out the class puppet, Juan. Ask him *¿Qué hiciste ayer durante el recreo?* (What did you do yesterday breaktime?) Answer for him: for example, *Durante el recreo, jugué el futbol.* (At breaktime I played football.) Mime the action.

- Teach other answers. For example: … *comí una manzana* (I ate an apple); *canté* (I sang); *trabajé* (I worked); *hablé con mi amigo* (I talked to my friend).

- Test the children's memories as you say one of the sentences about what you did at breaktime. Can the children mime the action?

- Ask the children to think what they did at breaktime yesterday. Can they tell their talk partner in Spanish? Will their partner mime the correct action?

- With the children, write a timetable for what you did at breaktime each day last week. For example:

    Lunes comí un plátano. (Monday I ate a banana.)
    Martes…

- Read the timetable together as the children perform the actions.

- Put the children into groups of five, each to take one day of last week. Encourage group collaboration as each child writes and practises a sentence stating what they did.

- Watch and listen to each group's human breaktime timetable. Which week was the most fun?

Follow-up
Ask the children to create their own, new breaktime timetable for last week. Discuss formats and suggest the title *La semana pasada* (Last week). Encourage pictures as well as writing.

In Spanish state schools, children do not wear a school uniform.

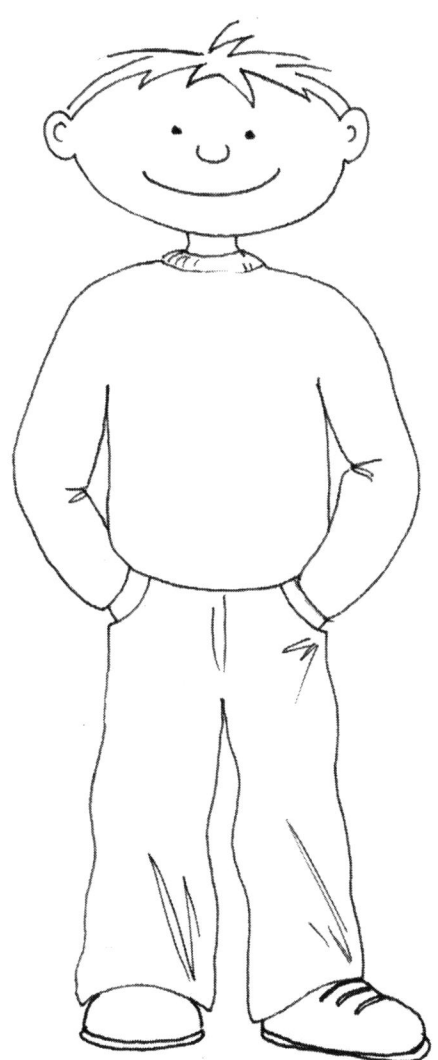

¿Qué hiciste durante el recreo?

For each picture, copy the sentence that says what I did.
You will have to complete some.

Ayudé_____   Comí.
Jugué al hockey.   Trabajé.
Canté.   Hablé con mis amigos.
Jugué al   Bebí.
_____

More ideas for...

Work at school

- Practice the pronunciation of *c*. Usually, it is a hard sound as in 'cat'. However, in words where *c* is followed by *i* or *e*, the *c* sound is soft, like 'th' in 'think'.

- Add reality to this unit's theme by making contact with a partner school in a Spanish-speaking country. (Your local town may be twinned with a town in Spain.) Set up email contact so the children can inform one another about life in their respective schools. Suggest the schools exchange photographs of their schools. Pictures annotated by their Spanish-speaking counterparts will provide the children with an interesting, discussion-provoking classroom display.

- Play **The gender game**. Make a large cardboard dice and label each face: *patio; aparcamiento; entrada; clase; cocina; salón de actos;* and *biblioteca*. Roll the dice and invite the children to decide whether the resulting noun is *masulino* or *femenino*. Encourage the children to use both the definite and indefinite article each time: for example, *el patio, un patio*.

- Make a new large cardboard dice and label each face either *masulino* or *femenino*. Roll the dice as previously, but this time challenge the children to think of a suitable school noun.

- Extend your work on time by making a display of three clock faces.

  ○ Draw the hands of the first clock at 10 o'clock and write *Son las diez*.

  ○ Draw the hands of the third clock at 11 o'clock and write *Son las once*.

  ○ Label the times on the middle clock at five minute intervals: *Son las diez y cinco/diez/veinte/ veinticinco. Son las once menos veinticinco/veinte/ diez/cinco.* Include half-hours and quarter-hours

- Give the children a copy of 'The timetable song' from Lesson 3. Ask them to write a second verse, repeating the five days but with new verbs and subjects. Make sure the children have access to a bank of relevant vocabulary and bilingual dictionaries.

Work at home

- Give the children photocopiable 19A . Suggest they improve their Spanish spelling and word recognition by playing the games from Lesson 2 with someone at home.

- Ask the children to draw a plan of their real (or ideal) school. Give them photocopiable 19A to use the vocabulary to label the plan. Are there places and vocabulary they want to add?

- Suggest the children think about what they would like to learn about Spanish school life. Then they could write a set of questions in English to send to a child in a Spanish-speaking school. Point out the need to keep the language of the questions clear and simple.

- Give the children the sentences only from photocopiable 19B . Ask them to draw a picture and write the English translation for each.

Spanish schoolchildren have a very long summer holiday. It lasts from mid-June to mid-September!

¡Uno, dos, tres!

Unit 20 – Nuestro mundo

(Our world)

Unit theme
The world

Teaching points
- Identifying and naming continents
- Making statements about rivers of the world
- Forecasting the weather
- Using a non-fiction text

Grammar
- Simple superlatives, eg *el/la más grande*
- Expressing the immediate future: *ir a* + infinitive (*Va a hacer sol,* etc)

Language sounds
- -ca

Vocabulary

Europa (f)	Europe
América del sur (f)	South America
América del norte (f)	North America
Asia (f)	Asia
Oceania (f)	Australasia
África (f)	Africa
Antártida (f)	Antarctica
el/la más grande	the biggest (m/f)
Va a hacer buen tiempo	It's going to be fine (weather)
Va a llover	It's going to rain
Va a nevar	It's going to snow
Va a hacer viento	It's going to be windy
el Nilo	the Nile
el Ródano	the Rhône
el Danubio	the Danube
el Rin	the Rhine
el Yangtsé	the Yangtze
el Amazonas	the Amazon
el Támesis	the Thames
el Ebro	the Ebro
la desembocadura	the mouth of the river
el río desemboca en el mar/océano	the river flows out to the sea/ocean
el nacimiento	the source
un lago	a lake
una montaña	a mountain
los altiplanos	the high plateaux
la selva tropical	the rainforest
un valle	a valley
una ciénaga	a swamp
una cascada	a waterfall
una ciudad	a city
el océano	the ocean
otra información	other information

Additional vocabulary for teachers

¿En qué continente está …?	In which continent is …?
¿Qué tiempo va a hacer?	What's the weather going to be like?
En este actividad sois exploradores	For this activity you are explorers
Nuestro viaje va a empezar en agosto	Our journey is going to start in August
Vamos a explorar el/la …	We're going to explore the …

Resources
A globe, atlases and a world map

Lesson 1 Nuestro mundo fantástico (Our fantastic world)

Resources:
A globe; atlases; a world map; unnamed continent outlines

- Use a globe to identify and name the continents: *Europa, África, América del sur, América del norte, Asia, Oceania, África, Antártida.*

- Keep to oral work as the children practise pronunciation of the continent names in **Follow my leader**: you vary the way you say the names (fast/slowly/quietly/loudly); the children repeat them in the same way.

- Display outline shapes of continents. Challenge the children to name them in Spanish.

- Repeat these names: *África, América del sur, América del norte.*

- Write -*ca* on the whiteboard. Ask the children to memorise the grapheme. Cover it up. Can partners write the grapheme in the air? Can they write it on their mini-whiteboard? Reveal your writing: is everyone correct?

- Ask the children what other words they know ending –*ca*. (*el música* (music), *la física* (physics), *la roca* (rock), *cómica* (comical).

- Let the children try writing the continents' names before you display the written forms. Do the children think they are getting better at writing Spanish sounds they hear?

- Explain that rivers of the world are important in this unit. Ask the children to tell their partner, in English, two. Can they name four between them? Share results.

- Display this list of Spanish names of important world rivers: *el Amazonas; el Danubio; el Ganges; el Nilo; el Rin; el Yangtsé; el Ebro; el Támesis.*

- Locate the rivers on a globe or atlas: for example, *Aquí está…el Nilo* (Here is…the Nile).

Follow-up
Give the children an unmarked map of the world. Ask them to label its continents and identify three rivers.

Lesson 2 Los ríos del mundo (Rivers of the world)

Resources:
A globe; atlases; a world map; unnamed continent outlines

- Revise the names of continents and rivers from Lesson 1:

  ○ Show or draw in the air the shapes of continents for the children to name.

  ○ Read through the list of important world rivers together.

- On a world map, identify the Yangtze and say *El Yangtsé está en Asia*. Locate other rivers on the list and help the children to construct similar sentences stating their continent.

- Enlarge, display and read aloud Part 1 of photocopiable 20A, pausing regularly so children can point to where you have reached.

- Read the text again. Ask English comprehension questions:

  ○ Which rivers are mentioned?

  ○ Which river is talked about most?

  ○ Can you find one fact given about that river?

- Encourage partner discussion before you share answers as a class.

- Read the text again as the children follow. Point out facts and names the children have mentioned. Underline *él* in the text (used four times). Can the children work out why *él* is used? (It is a pronoun standing in place of *el Amazonas*. Its use avoids too much repetition of the river's name.) Point out that the pronoun *él* has an accent; the definite article *el* does not.

- Ask *¿En qué continente está el Amazonas?* Invite the children to write the answer on their mini-whiteboard. Compare results. Accept *El Amazonas está en América del sur* but encourage *Él está en América del sur.*

- Ask the same question about the Thames: *¿El Támesis, él está en que continente?* Ask the children to answer with a pronoun (*Él está en Europa.*)

Follow-up
Put the children into pairs to question and answer each other about the rivers and the continents they are in.

Remind them to be careful to use the correct pronoun. After oral practice, they should each write three questions and their answers, using pronouns.

Lesson 3 ¿Qué tiempo va a hacer? (What is the weather going to be like?)

Resources:
Weather symbols; a globe; a world map; six large, cardboard cubes with weather symbols on the faces

- Display and read aloud the text from Lesson 2.

- Explain that you want to extract the important information in Spanish from the text. Give the children a facts chart made up of two columns. In the first column, have these headings:
  1. Nombre del rio 2. La longitud 3. Su nacimiento 4. La desembocadura 5. Otra información

- Ask partners to work out what the headings mean before agreeing as a class. (1. Name of the river 2. Length 3. Source 4. Mouth of river 5. Other information)

- Ask the partners to fill in the second column in Spanish by reading the text carefully. Check answers as a class. What *Otra información* was picked out?

- Make a display of weather symbols, point to one and ask ¿Qué tiempo hace? (What's the weather like?) Let partners give each other an answer before you accept an answer from the class.

- Say and write this question: ¿Qué tiempo va a hacer mañana? (What is the weather going to be like tomorrow?) Point out that the question is about the future and is expressed by the verb *ir (va)* followed by *a* and an infinitive (*hacer*).

- Let the children become weather forecasters and answer your question with *Va a…*

- Make the children form a large circle around you. Use a large dice, a weather symbol on each face. Ask about the future weather somewhere on the globe, for example: ¿Qué tiempo va a hacer en Inglaterra? Toss the cube: whoever catches it must forecast the weather on the top face. (For example: *En Inglaterra va a llover.*)

- Make more cubes and divide the class into groups of six for the children to play the game. Make sure that everyone makes a forecast.

Follow-up
Give the children photocopiable 20B. Explain that the female explorer is going to follow the course of a river. She wants to know what the weather will be like in these places when she is there.

Lesson 4 Vamos a explorar (We're going to explore)

Resources:
Photocopiable 20B; the children's work from the **Follow-up** Lesson 3

- Return the children's weather forecasts (photocopiable 20B, **Follow-up** Lesson 3) and let some children read theirs out.

- Explain that the features on photocopiable 20B are all likely scenery at stages of a river's journey. Have the children other scenery suggestions (in English) to add?

- Share ideas and write on the whiteboard *un lago, un desierto, una cascada, el mar, el océano*. Suggest adding these features' pictures or symbols to photocopiable 20B.

- Invite the children to join you on a journey tracking your imaginary river. Announce *Vamos a explorar el Zukoro.* (We're going to explore the Zukoro.) The children must help you write about the start of the journey along your imaginary river.

- Write a text together. Make sure you keep using the river's name. For example:

  ○ *Vamos a explorar el Zukoro. El Zukoro está en Asia. El Zukoro es el río más largo de Asia. El Zukoro tiene 5,500 kilómetros de largo. El nacimiento del Zukoro está en Pakistán, en las montañas. EL Zukoro pasa por los valles. En agosto en los valles va a hacer viento.*

  ○ *(We are going to explore the Zukoro. The Zukoro is in Asia. The Zukoro is the longest river in Asia. The Zukoro is 5,500km long. The source of the Zukoro is in Pakistán, in the mountains. In August in the mountains it's going to be windy.)*

- Read your text together. Do the children notice the name's repetition? What would be better? (Some use of the pronoun *él.*) Make these changes and save this model text.

- Put the children into pairs to map the route of their own imaginary river. Suggest showing their river's course on a poster; in separate pictures; or in a power point presentation

- Partners will make an oral presentation to an audience, so they must prepare a written sentence for each stage of the river's journey.

- Let the children practise before they make their presentation to others.

Follow-up

Explain that the children, as explorers, will make a journey of four or five months as they explore the track of their imaginary river. Using the class model text as an example and still in pairs, they must write a similar paragraph about any month and stage of their planned journey.

Los ríos del mundo

Cada continente tiene un gran río. El Ródano está en Europa. Hay el Nilo en África. En América del sur hay el Amazonas. Él es el segundo río más largo del mundo aparte del Nilo. El Amazonas tiene 6,440 kilómetros de longitud. Su nacimiento está en las montañas de Perú. Él pasa por las ciénagas en Brasil. Por fin, él desemboca en el océano Atlántico.

PART 2

Each continent has a big river. The Rhône is in Europe. There is the Nile in Africa. In South America there is the Amazon. It is the second-biggest river in the world after the Nile. The Amazon is 6,440km long. Its source is in the mountains of Peru. It flows through Brazil. Finally, it flows out into the Atlantic Ocean.

Nombre del río	
La longitud	
Su nacimiento	
La desembocadura	
Otra información	

¿Qué tiempo va a hacer?

Weather phrases:

Va a...

hacer sol   hacer viento
hacer calor   llover
hacer frío   hacer mal tiempo
   nevar

Give the river explorer a written forecast for each month. For example:

En julio en las montañas va a hacer frío.

julio *las montañas*	**agosto** *los altiplanos*	**septiembre** *la selva tropical*

octubre *los valles*	**noviembre** *una ciudad*	**diciembre** *las ciénagas*
	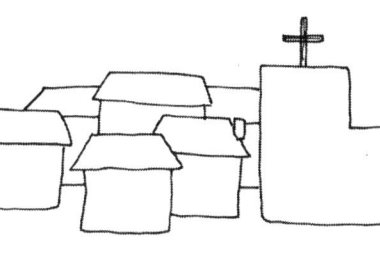	

More ideas for...

Work at school

- After the children have done the English comprehension questions in the first **Work at home** activity, give them a copy of that text, 'El Támesis' and part 3 of photocopiable 20A so they can complete the facts table (in Spanish) about the text.

- Create a weather corner, with the headings **Hoy** (Today) and **Mañana** (Tomorrow). Choose a different pair of children each day to:

  ○ select a weather symbol and write a weather report of today's weather (in present tense);

  ○ select a weather symbol and write a weather forecast for tomorrow's weather (immediate future tense, using *ir a* + infinitive).

- Refer to the children's presentation in Lesson 4 and their written work in the **Follow-up**. Ask them to write a similar text about a different month and stage as they explore the track of their imaginary river.

Work at home

- Write and give the children a copy of this text:

  ### El Támesis

  El Támesis es un rio muy importante en Inglaterra. Él es 338 kilómetros de largo. El nacimiento del Támesis está cerca de Cirencester y el río pasa por Londres, la capital de Inglaterra. Él desemboca por fin en el Mar del Norte.

- Set the children these English comprehension questions to answer in English:

  ○ Which river is talked about?

  ○ What country is it in?

  ○ Where is the river's source?

  ○ Does the river go near London?

  ○ Can you find one other fact given about the river?

- Ask the children to write a translation of the text used in the previous activity.

  (The Thames
  The Thames is a very important river in England. It is 338km long. Its source is near Cirencester and the river runs through London, the capital of England. Finally, it flows into the North Sea.)

- Ask the children to find six rivers in Spain. Can they write their names in Spanish and English?

The Ebro is Spain's longest river. It flows for 910 km. The upper part of the Ebro River basin, the Rioja Alta, gives its name to the Rioja wine produced there.

Unit 21 – Crear una cafetería

(Creating a café)

Unit theme
Food and drinks

Teaching points
- Food and drink quantities
- Making a café transaction
- Checking the meaning

Grammar
- Preterite verb tense: third person singular (*comió; bebió*)
- Peposition: *de*

Language sounds
- Using phoneme-grapheme correspondence to work out the pronunciation of new words
- *ai* (as in *vainilla*)
- *ll, o, c, ch, ó* and silent *h*

Vocabulary

un agua mineral	a mineral water
un chocolate caliente	a hot chocolate
un café solo	a (black) coffee
un café con leche	a coffee with milk
un batido	a milkshake
una taza de té	a cup of tea
una limonada	a lemonade
una coca-cola	a cola
una bolsa de patatas fritas	a packet of crisps
una ración de patatas fritas	a portion of chips
una pizza	a pizza
Comió...	He/she ate ...
Bebió...	He/she drank ...
un helado de chocolate/ fresa/ vainilla	a chocolate/ strawberry/ vanilla ice cream
No entiendo	I don't understand
¿Puede repetir, por favor?	Can you repeat, please?
¡Que aproveche!	Enjoy your meal!
un sándwich tostado	a toasted sandwich
una tortilla	a potato omelette
un perrito caliente	a hot dog
una ensalada mixta	a mixed salad
una horchata	a milky almond drink
turrón/caramelo/piña/ pistacho/almendra	nougat/caramel/ pineapple/ pistachio/almond
Tengo	I have
¿Cuánto es?	How much is it?
por favor	please
¿Que desea?	What would you like?

Additional vocabulary for teachers

¿Qué comiste/bebiste ayer?	What did you have to eat/drink yesterday?
¿Qué comió/bebió ayer?	What did he/she eat/drink yesterday?
los helados (m plural)	the ice creams
las tapas (f plural)	the snacks
las bebidas (f plural)	the drinks
¿Qué hay en la carta?	What is on the menu?
un vaso	a glass
un litro	a litre
una cuchara de sopa	a soup spoon
una cucharilla	a teaspoon
al gusto	according to taste
Tomar frío	Eat/drink chilled
En inglés se dice ...	In English we say ...

Resources
Pictures of Spanish cafés

Lesson 1 La carta (The menu)

Resources:
A picture of a typical Spanish café; individual copies of photocopiable 21A, part 1; an enlarged copy of photocopiable 21A, part 1

- Display a picture of a typical Spanish café. In English, ask: What sort of place is this? Have you been to a Spanish café? What was it like? Did it differ from English cafés?

- Display an enlarged copy of part 1, photocopiable 21A. Explain that the words and prices are from a Spanish café's menu.

- Put the children into pairs with a copy of part 1, photocopiable 21A. Ask them to mark the words with three colours to represent:

  ○ words they know;

  ○ words they can probably guess;

  ○ words they do not know.

- As a class, compare results and strategies used to guess meanings.

- Make a list on the whiteboard of unknown words (without saying them). Put the children into pairs with a dictionary. Challenge them to find and write quickly the meanings. Can they use their existing knowledge of phoneme-grapheme correspondence to work out how to pronounce the new words?

- Share ideas and help the children with correct prounciation.

- Bring out Juan, the class puppet. He always chooses lunch from this café's menu!

- Using the preterite tense (see Unit 13) ask Juan: *¿Qué comiste ayer?* Through you, let him answer in the preterite tense: for example, *Comí una pizza*.

- Let the class ask the same question of you, your Teaching Assistant or an individual child. The person answering must say aloud *Comí* but only mouth the actual food. Will the class be able to identify the food?

- Play the game in pairs: one partner asking, the other saying and mouthing a reply. After three questions and answers, how many children identified all three mouthed foods? Did the speaker say the preterite tense correctly?

Follow-up
Supply these headings: *Los bocadillos* (Sandwiches); *Las tapas* (Snacks); *Los helados* (Ice cream); *Las bebidas frías* (Cold drinks); *Las bebidas calientes* (Hot drinks). Suggest the children sort and write the menu in these sections. Will the customer need any pictures?

Lesson 2 ¿Qué comiste ayer? (What did you eat yesterday?)

Resources:
An enlarged copy of photocopiable 21A, part 1

- Display the café menu (Lesson 1) suggesting the children ate here yesterday.

- Pose a question in the preterite tense: *¿Qué comiste ayer?* Let the children give an answer to a partner before you accept any. Write a correct answer on the whiteboard. For example: *Comí un sándwich tostado.*

- Demonstrate the third person singular form of the preterite tense by pointing to the child and saying: *Comió un sándwich.*

- Introduce the question *¿Qué bebiste ayer?* Let the children practise *Bebí ...* and *Bebió ...*

- Play **Trick or truth**:

  ○ Ask everyone to draw secretly on their mini-whiteboard something they ate or drank yesterday. Give everyone two voting cards: 'trick' and 'truth'.

  ○ When it is someone's turn to speak, they say an ate or drank sentence: for example, *Comí una ensalada mixta.*

  ○ The class votes on whether the person is saying the item they have drawn.

  ○ Count the votes, ask the person to show their picture and the class to state what is revealed: for example, *¡Comió una ración de patatas fritas!*

  ○ If most votes were wrong, the person wins a **Trick or truth** star.

  ○ Continue the game, moving between boy and girl speakers and using *Comí/Bebí* and *Comió/Bebió*.

- You and your Teaching Assistant take the roles of customer and ice cream seller. Encourage the children to help you with dialogue. Include:

A: *Buenos días, señor.*
B: *Buenos días …, ¿Qué desea?*
B: *Quiero un helado.*
B: *Tengo los helados de chocolate, de….*
A: *Un helado de….*
A: *¿Cuánto es?*
B: *……*

- Write an agreed dialogue on the whiteboard for the children, in pairs, to practise.

Follow-up
On one side of the whiteboard (preferably, an interactive whiteboard) draw four people named Miguel, Beatriz, Pedro, and Marta. On the other side, draw or write food and drinks. In the middle write *comió* and *bebió*. Ask the children to mix and match the people, verbs and foods to write sentences about who had what to eat or drink.

> Ice cream is often served with a glass of water. The water brings out the flavour of the ice cream.

Lesson 3 ¡Que aproveche! (Enjoy your food!)

Resources:
Cartons of ice cream; milk; sugar; powder flavouring; measuring jugs; mixing bowls; large glasses

- Read out the ingredients for a strawberry milkshake: *25cl de leche (*25 cl of milk); *2 cucharas de sopa de fresa en polvo* (2 soup spoons of strawberry powder)*; 2 cucharillas de azúcar extrafino (*2 teaspoons of caster sugar)*; 2 bolas de helado de vainilla* (2 scoops of vanilla ice cream).

- Say instructions as you mime making the drink: *Mezcla el leche, la fresa y el helado. Entonces añade el azúcar. (*Mix the milk, the strawberries and the ice cream and then add the sugar.)

- Repeat the instructions for the children to mime the actions.

- List new words on the whiteboard. Explain the meaning of *leche* with this sentence: *En inglés se dice 'milk' pero en español se dice 'leche'.* (In English we say 'milk' but in Spanish we say 'leche'.) Repeat this format for other ingredients and utensils, giving the children time to find the word listed and finish the sentence for you.

- Explain that the children are going to run a milkshake stall! Divide the class into groups. Have a range of ingredients and flavours available, groups deciding which one flavour milkshake to make on their stall. Encourage variety among the class. (Alternatively, let every group run an ice cream stall, on which they display the ice cream cone or wafer they have put together and have taster amounts available.)

- Set out the ingredients for children to take, measure, mix and make.

- Suggest that groups give their drink a name, for example *Chocolate Fantástico*.

- Have taster straws available so the children can sip a few milkshakes, recording their written opinion of each. (For example, *Chocolate Fantástico es delicioso.*)

- Compare verdicts and ask the children to award the drinks a score. Which stall was best?

Follow-up
Suggest the children create a poster to advertise their stall's products. Remind them to mention flavours and prices.

Lesson 4 La cafetería rara (The strange café)

Resources:
Individual copies of photocopiable 21B

- Give the children a copy of photocopiable 21B.

- Read through the playscript as the children follow.

- Discuss the meaning of the text. Ask the children: Why is the café strange? What does the waiter keep doing? Why is the customer surprised by the bill?

- Ask the children to identify an example of the preterite tense. (*Pedi*).

- Model reading and acting the play with your Teaching Assistant.

- Divide the class in half, perhaps boys and girls. Allocate the part of waiter to one half, the customer to the other.

- Let the class read the play, the children keeping to their parts. Encourage careful pronunciation and expressive voices and body language.

- Put the class into pairs to read the play. Let the class listen to and watch some performances.

- Suggest that this café and its waiter will go on being strange! Ask what changes could occur in a new script (different food, a different customer, different bill total).

- Ask the children, in pairs, to write a new script. Suggest they use photocopiable 21B as a model.

- Allow time for the children to practise reading and acting their play.

Follow-up
Let the children read and perform their plays for other members of the class.

In Spain it is usual to say ¡Que aproveche! (Enjoy your meal) to one another.

La carta

Part 1
Words:

Coca-cola 2,00 €
Batido 5,00 €
Café con leche 2,00 €
Café solo 1,50 €
bolsa de patatas fritas 1,50 €
Limonada 2,00 €
Agua mineral 2,50 €
Taza de té 3,00 €
Ración de patatas fritas 3,50 €
de chocolate/fresa/vainilla
Sándwich tostado de jamon 8,00 €
Tortilla 7,00 €
Zumo de naranja natural 3,00 €

Zumo de limón natural 3,00 €
Perrito caliente 8,50 €
de turrón/caramelo/piña/
pistacho/almendra
Pizza 7,00 €
Chocolate caliente 3,00 €
de jamon 7,00 €
de atún 7,00 €
Una bola 1,50 €
Dos bolas 3,00 €
Tres bolas 4,00 €
Zumo de naranja natural 3,00 €
Zumo de limón natural 3,00 €

Part 2
Likely grouping of words:

Los bocadillos
de queso
de jamón
de atún
Sándwich tostado de jamón

Tapas
Bolsa de patatas fritas
Ración de patatas fritas
Pizza
Tortilla
Perrito caliente

Helados
Una bola 1,50 €
Dos bolas 3,00 €
Tres bolas 4,00 €
de turrón/caramelo/piña/
pistacho/almendra /chocolate/
fresa/vainilla

Bebidas frías
Aqua mineral
Coca-cola
Batido

Limonada
Zumo de naranja natural 3,00 €
Zumo de limón natural 3,00 €

Bebidas calientes
Té
Café solo
Café con leche
Chocolate caliente

¡Uno, dos, tres!

La cafetería rara

EL CAMARERO: *Buenos días, señorita.*

LA SEÑORITA: *Buenos días, señor. La carta, por favor.*

EL CAMARERO: *Aquí tiene. ¿Qué desea?*

LA SEÑORITA: *Quiero un café con leche, un sándwich de queso, una bolsa de patatas fritas y un helado de chocolate.*

EL CAMARERO: *Aquí tiene un café de queso, un sándwich de café, una bolsa de chocolate et un helado de patatas fritas.*

LA SEÑORITA: *¡No! ¡No! Pedí un café con leche, un sándwich de queso, una bolsa de patatas fritas y un helado de chocolate.*

EL CAMARERO: *Si señorita. Aquí tiene un café de queso, un sándwich de café, una bolsa de chocolate et un helado de patatas fritas.*

LA SEÑORITA: *¡Puaj! ¿Cuánto es?*

EL CAMARERO: *¡Sesenta euros!*

LA SEÑORITA: *¿Sesenta euros? ¡Es una cafetería rara!*

- -

The strange café

WAITER: *Hello, miss.*

GIRL: *Hello. The menu please.*

WAITER: *Here you are. What would you like?*

GIRL: *I'd like a coffee with milk, a cheese sandwich, a portion of chips and a chocolate ice cream.*

WAITER: *Here you are: a cheese coffee, a coffee sandwich, a portion of chocolate and a chips ice cream.*

GIRL: *No! No! I ordered a coffee with milk, a cheese sandwich, a portion of chips and a chocolate ice cream.*

WAITER: *Yes, miss. Here you are: a cheese coffee, a coffee sandwich, a portion of chocolate and a chips ice cream.*

GIRL: *Yuck! How much is it?*

WAITER: *Sixty euros!*

GIRL: *Sixty euros? This is a strange café!*

More ideas for...

Work at school

- Display a map of Spain and point out its division into regions. Identify some regions: for example, Valencia, Andalucía, Cataluña, the Basque Country. Ask the children to use the internet to find out about food popular in each region.

- Extend the customer/seller dialogue in Lesson 2 to include strategies for dealing with situations when you do not understand what is being said. Suggest the use of *No entiendo* (I don't understand) and *¿Puede repetir, por favor?* (Will you repeat that please?) Let the children try them out in an adapted version of the paired dialogue.

- Set up a café board in your Spanish corner of the classroom. Write on it a changing, short menu of today's foods and drinks. Include new words and encourage partners to read them to each other. Can the children use their knowledge of phoneme-grapheme correspondence to work out the words' pronunciation. Are there clues to their meanings?

Work at home

- Give the children part 1 of photocopiable 21A. Suggest they use it to help them write a bilingual menu (Spanish on one half, English on the other) for their own new café. What special foods will they have? Will their prices be sensible? How tempting will their menu look?

- Ask the children to find out about euros. When was this currency introduced? Which countries use it? Is it worth more or less than the English pound?

- Suggest the children draw a food map of Spain. They should have regions marked in different colours. Each region should have a picture or name of a food or drink popular in that area.

- Give the children a copy of the dialogue in Lesson 2, between a customer and the ice cream seller. Ask the children to use it as a model as they write their own dialogue between the café owner and a customer, as the customer orders something to eat or drink.

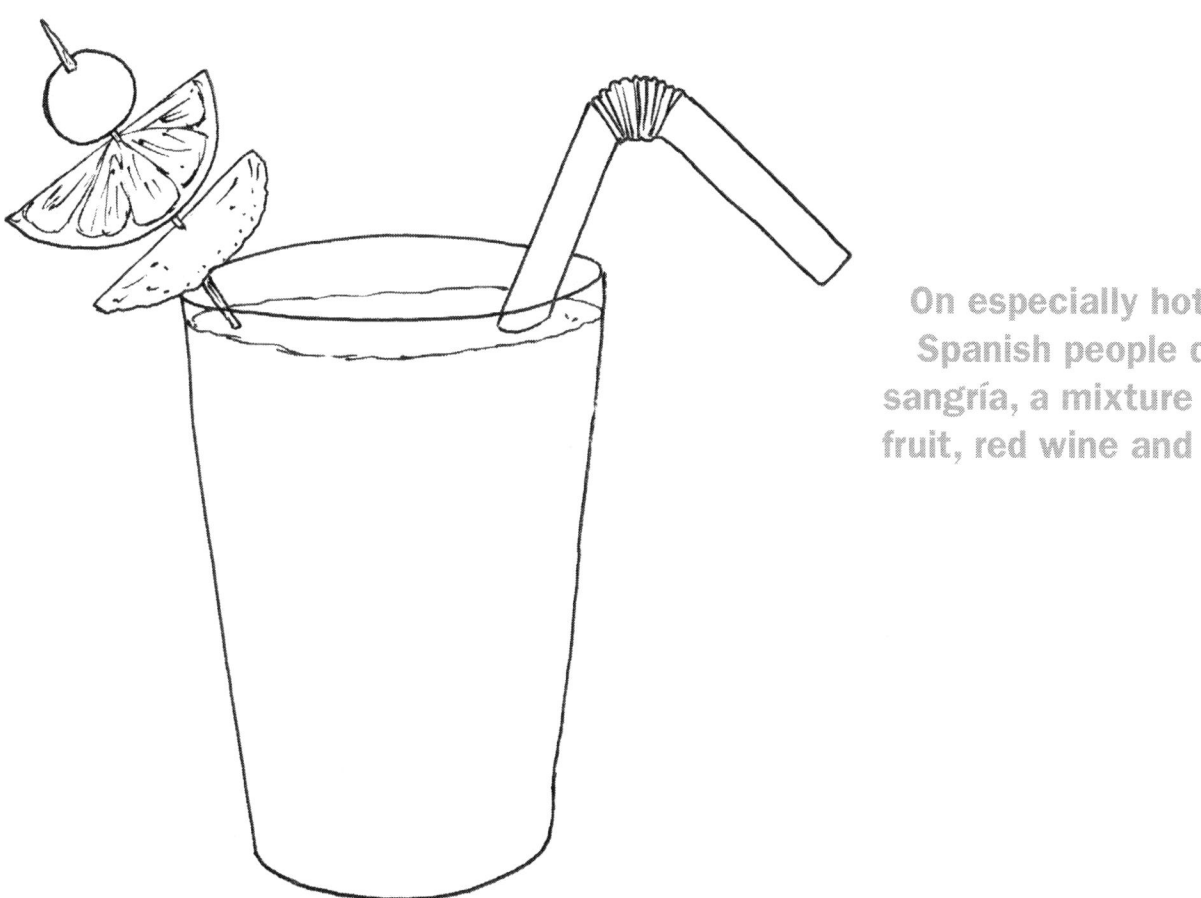

On especially hot days, Spanish people drink sangría, a mixture of ice, fruit, red wine and water.

¡Uno, dos, tres!

Unit 22 – El pasado y el presente

(Then and now)

Unit theme
Towns - then and now

Teaching points
- Describing a town
- Comparing a settlement today with one in the past
- Writing a guide for tourists
- Using numbers
- Saying the year

Grammar
- Antonyms
- Imperfect verb tense: *haber (había)* and *ser (era)*
- *Mucho/mucha; muchos/muchas*
- *Poco/poca; pocos/pocas*

Vocabulary

el/un supermercado	the/a supermarket
la/una panadería	the/a bakery
la/una carnicería	the/a butcher's
la/una pastelería	the/a cake shop
la/una pescadería	the/a fishmonger's
la/una tienda de comestibles	the/a grocer's
Había…	There was/were…
Era…	It was…
hoy	today
mucho	a lot (of)
poco	few
veinte	20
veintiuno, veintidós	21–22
treinta	30
cuarenta	40
cincuenta	50
sesenta	60
setenta	70
ochenta	80
noventa	90
cien	100
mil	1,000
animado/animada	lively (m/f)
tranquilo/tranquila	calm (m/f)
precioso/preciosa	beautiful (m/f)
moderno/moderna	modern (m/f)
viejo/vieja	old (m/f)
feo/fea	ugly (m/f)

Additional vocabulary for teachers

No había…	There wasn't/weren't any…
Nació en…	He/she was born in…
entonces	at that time/then

Resources
Photographs or pictures of places in your local town.

Lesson 1 En la ciudad (In the town)

Resources:
Recognisable symbols of familiar town places; a prepared list of places in and absent from local town

- Display recognisable symbols for familiar town places: a shop, café, market, train station, post office and a library. Agree in English what the places are.

- On the whiteboard, write the first letter of each equivalent Spanish noun (*una tienda, una cafetería, un mercado, una estación de trenes, una oficina de correos, una biblioteca*) but only dashes for the other letters: for example: *un m——; una c——*.

- Tell the children that this is a memory test: these are words they should know! (Refer to Unit 15.)

- Challenge them to remember three of the words, silently, list them, and compare results with a partner. Can they remember five or six of the words between them?

- Share results as a class and write the missing letters on the whiteboard.

- Hold up a symbol and ask, for example, *¿Es una cafetería?* for a child to answer *Sí, es una cafetería* or *No, es un/una ...*

- As you question children and they answer, encourage the class to listen carefully. Can they distinguish between your intonation (a question) and the child's (a statement)?

- Play **Up or down?** Pick up a place symbol and ask the class *¿Es un mercado?* However, make your intonation the flat intonation of a statement. The class should refuse to answer you! They should only answer your questions when your intonation rises correctly. How many children get caught answering at the wrong time? Let individual children take your place at trying to catch the class out.

- Apply the place vocabulary to your local town and say and write a sentence: for example, *En Warwick, hay un mercado.* What Spanish sentence can the children work out?

- Draw four places on the whiteboard, ticks next to three, a cross by the fourth. Write a statement: for example, *En Warwick, hay un mercado, una cafetería y un museo, pero no hay panadería.* (In Warwick, there is a market, a café and a museum, but there is no bakery.) Point out the negative *no hay*. Leave this sentence on the whiteboard.

- Play **Tourist trail**: two children (tourists) leave the room; the rest of the class agree on three places for their imaginary town; when the tourists return to the room, they try to identify the places, asking for example: *¿Hay un museo?* The townspeople chorus a reply. Limit the number of questions allowed (perhaps six). How many places will the tourists identify?

Follow-up
Return to the long statement about Warwick (*En Warwick, hay un mercado, una cafetería y un museo, pero no hay panadería*). Remind the children about the negative. Draw new sets of symbols on the board with three ticks and a cross for the children to create new long statements.

Lesson 2 El pasado y el presente (Then and now)

Resources:
Six small foam balls; a current picture of a town and a picture of the same town in about 1948

- Revise numbers. (See Units 1, 2, 9 and 12, Book 1.) Do oral practice, the class counting up to 30. Explain that after thirty, they must simply add *y* plus the additional number. Give examples: *treinta y dos* (32); *cuarenta y tres* (43); *cincuenta y cinco* (55).

- Play **Toss a ten**, the children, in circles of five with a ball: one group member says 10 and throws the ball; the catcher says the next multiple of 10. Can they reach 100? Can they play the game backwards?

- Write on the whiteboard 1948. Ask the children, in pairs, to decide how to say the year in Spanish (*mil novecientos cuarenta y ocho*). Let them try 1965 (*mil novecientos sesenta y cinco*).

- Explain that *dos mil* is used once the date reaches 2000. Write on the board *dos mil diez*. Can the children work out the year? (2010)

- Remind the children that this unit is about past and present towns. Display two pictures: a town in about 1948 and the same town in the present time. Above one picture write, for example, *En 1948*; above the other, *Hoy*.

- Concentrate on the modern scene, using sentences such as: *Hay tres supermercados. Hay una carnicería.* Write the sentences on the whiteboard. Ask what the sentences have in common. (*Hay*) What does the word mean? (There is/are)

- Move to the picture of the past. Explain that *Hay* must now become *Había*. Can the children guess what it means? (There was/were)

Follow-up

Display these statements. Ask the children to copy them, each time adding a statement about the town today. Afterwards, they must decide how to link each pair: with *y* (and) or *pero* (but). For example: *En 1948, había una carnicería* **pero** *hoy, hay un supermercado.*

1. *En 1948, había una carnicería.*
2. *En 1948, había una pescadería.*
3. *En 1948, había una iglesia moderna.*
4. *En 1948, había un colegio pequeño.*
5. *En 1948, había una estación de trenes.*

Lesson 3 ¡Salut! (Hello!)

Resources:
Individual copies of part 1, photocopiable 22A and one enlarged copy; a slide show of images for your interactive whiteboard, or drawn pictures for the whiteboard (for **Follow-up**)

- Tell the children that you have found – on a Spanish internet website - a description of people's local town.

- Give the children a copy of the text (part 1 of photocopiable 22A). Put them into pairs to try to make sense of the text. Advise they:

  ○ highlight words/phrases they know;

  ○ read parts aloud.

- Let pairs double up to pool ideas and share findings.

- Display on the whiteboard an enlarged copy of the text, reading it aloud as the children follow. Question them about meaning. What was easy to understand? Why?

- Agree that the text describes the town in the present and in the past. The first paragraph has the present tense verbs *hay* and *es*. What are the past tense verbs in the second paragraph? (*había* and *era*)

- Did the children identify and understand many adjectives in the text? Ask children to come to the whiteboard and identify an adjective. Highlight some of them: *preciosa; pequeña; animada*. What is noticeable about the highlighted adjectives? (They all end in *a*.)

- Write this on the whiteboard: *El colegio es viejo. La tienda es vieja.* Can the children explain why *viejo* becomes *vieja*? (*El colegio* is masculine: *la tienda* is feminine.)

- Work through all the adjectives in the text, giving partners time to confer before you agree on the spelling and pronunciation of their singular masculine and feminine forms (*grande/grande; animado/animada; precioso/preciosa; moderno/moderna; útil/útil; viejo/vieja; diferente/diferente; pequeño/pequeña; tranquilo/tranquila.*

- Agree on a mime for each of the preceding adjectives. Play two games:

  ○ **Synonyms** When you call out an adjective, the children mime the appropriate action.

  ○ **Antonyms** When you call out an adjective, the children mime the opposite. Can anyone say the Spanish opposite?

Follow-up
Give the children, in pairs, a jumbled bank of about 20 adjectives to agree on their meanings and action mimes. In a partner game of **Antonyms**, who scores best at miming the opposite action? What about saying the antonym?

Lesson 4 Los turistas (The tourists)

Resources:
An enlarged copy of part 1, photocopiable 22A; individual copies of photocopiable 22B; a current picture of your town and one taken in about 1948

- Remind the children about the Spanish town information (part 1, photocopiable 22A).

- Display and investigate the text in more detail. Help the children identify places mentioned.

- Point out important sentence constructions, and adjectives (See Lesson 3).

- Write *mucho* and *poco* on the whiteboard and define them. Highlight other forms of these words in the text: *mucha, muchas, muchos* and *pocos*. Explain that their word ending changes to agree with the noun. Create a slide show of images for your interactive whiteboard and pairs of phrases or sentences. For each, ask the children to decide which to use: for example, a picture of a big bunch of bananas needs the sentence *Hay muchos plátanos*; the picture of only a few bananas, *Hay pocos plátanos*.

- Tell the children your idea: a tourist information leaflet about their town! Display past and present pictures of the town. Discuss paper leaflets and an on-screen version for the school website.

- Give the children photocopiable 22B to write their word bank and notes as they plan their leaflet.

- Encourage the children to show their plans to someone else and ask for comments. (If children prefer to work with a partner, they could ask another pair for feedback.)

- Suggest the children follow the three-step writing routine: 1 Plan. 2 Do. 3 Review.

- After planning, they do their written draft. They exchange with someone else and receive their comments before they review and re-write their text and create a leaflet with illustrations – by hand or on computer with publishing software.

Follow-up

Let the children pretend to be tourists and read one another's leaflets. Encourage positive feedback as they tell one another what they enjoyed. What made them enthusiastic about exploring the town?

You will probably find a weekly market in any town you visit in Spain. It's a good place to buy fresh food.

¡Hola! Os describo mi ciudad

El presente
Hoy, …es una ciudad muy grande. Es también una ciudad muy animada. Hay mucha gente, muchas tiendas y muchos coches. Hay restaurantes, cafeterías y cuatro supermercados. Hay una biblioteca preciosa y muchas casas modernas. La biblioteca es muy útil. Hay también un parque. Nuestro colegio es bastante viejo y está al lado del parque.

El pasado
En 1948, … la ciudad era muy diferente. Era más pequeña y era menos animada. Había pocos coches y el centro de la ciudad era más tranquilo. Había muchas tiendas pequeñas – una carnicería, una tienda de comestibles y cuatro panaderías. No había restaurante pero había dos cafeterías. ¡En 1948, nuestro colegio era moderno!

Hello! Let me present my town to you

Now
Today, … it is a very large town. It is also a very lively town. There are many people, many shops and many cars. There are restaurants, cafés and four supermarkets. There is a beautiful library and many modern houses. The library is very useful. There is also a park. Our school is quite old and is next to the park.

Then
In 1948, the town was very different. It was smaller and less lively. There were few cars and the town
centre was more peaceful. There were many small shops – a butcher's, a grocer's, and
four bakeries. There was no restaurant but there were two cafés. In 1948, our school was modern!

El plan

Vocabulary

Places

Adjectives

Important verbs and phrases

Contents

Proposed illustrations

Opening words

More ideas for...

Work at school

- Make this unit an opportunity to establish or reinforce links with a school in a Spanish-speaking country. The children will be able to exchange information about their towns and gain further insight into Spanish life and culture.

- Reinforce the distinction between the speech intonation of a statement and a question by playing games of **Juan dice** ('Simon says'). The children mime the action said only if they hear a statement; they do nothing if they hear a question. For example, *¡Abre la boca!* (Open your mouth!) produces a mime; *¿Abre la boca?* (Open your mouth?) produces nothing.

- Ask the children to design a symbol for each of the individual shops likely to be in towns of the past or present. Suggest that the symbol should be easily identifiable. The children could provide a key at the bottom of the page.

- Put the children into small groups. Assign a Spanish shop to each group to create shop windows for a class mural. Agree on shop order and numbering, *setenta y tres* (73) onwards. When the display is complete, use it for oral number practice, asking questions such as *¿La pescadería, qué número es?* (What number is the fishmonger's?)

Work at home

- Give the children a list of Spanish shops and town buildings. Ask the children to match them with the jumbled English list.

- Give the children a copy of part 1, photocopiable 22A. Suggest they are being paid to translate the text into English. How well can they do?

- Set spelling homework with a difference, choosing vocabulary linked to this unit. Give the children a list of Spanish shops to learn their gender and spelling. Advise them to use the **Look, Say, Cover, Write, Check** method.

In Spain, it is common for the market stallholders to let you try some of the food they are selling.

¡Uno, dos, tres!

Unit 23 – En el parque de atracciones

(At the theme park)

Unit theme
The theme park

Teaching points
- Talking about a visit to a theme park, referring to the past
- Using adjectives to add detail and interest
- Expressing an opinion

Grammar
- Preterite verb tense: *ir (fui)*; m*ontar (monté)*; *ver (vi)*; *oír (oí)*

Language sounds
- é

Vocabulary

un parque de atracciones	a theme park
emocionante	exciting
espantoso	frightening
rápido	fast
extraordinario	amazing
gracioso	funny
fantástico	great/fantastic
mágico	magical
Fui …	I went …
Monté en el tren fantasma	I went for a ride on the ghost train
Vi …	I saw …
Oí …	I heard …
el tiovivo	the merry-go-round
el tren fantasma	the ghost train
la montaña rusa	the rollercoaster
la noria	the big wheel
una entrada para	one ticket for
estatura mínima	minimum height
edad mínima	minimum age
Hay que tener una estatura de …	You should be … tall
Hay que tener … años	You should be … years old
un esqueleto	a skeleton
un búho	an owl
un lobo	a wolf
una puerta	a door
una bruja	a witch
las cadenas	chains
las ratas	rats

Additional vocabulary for teachers

Vamos a visitar un parque de atracciones	We are going to visit a theme park
una atracción	a (theme park) ride
mi atracción favorita	my favourite ride
Cuesta … euros	That costs … euros
también	also

Resources
Pictures of and information about theme parks here and in Spanish-speaking countries

¡Uno, dos, tres!

Lesson 1 Las atracciones (The rides)

Resources:
Pictures of theme-park rides; individual copies of photocopiable 23A; a computer and internet access

- Introduce the subject of theme parks. Ask the children to name, in English, some traditional theme park rides.

- Show pictures, and sketch and list four rides on the whiteboard: *la noria; el tiovivo; el tren fantasma; la montaña rusa*. Encourage actions and vary your voice (quiet to loud, sad to happy) the children repeating the names in the same way.

- Beside each ride's name, write a price: for example, *5.50€. (cinco euros cincuenta)*.

- Ask questions about the prices: for example, *La noria, ¿cuánto cuesta?*

- Suggest the children write a secret price list for the rides on their individual whiteboard. Partners ask the prices of rides, writing down the answers they hear. When they reveal their answers to each other, do they match the prices?

- Return to your price list on the whiteboard. Add further writing to the prices with an age or height restriction. For example: *Hay que tener una estatura de 1m 20. Hay que tener ocho años.* (You must be 1m 20 tall. You must be eight years old.)

- Ask the children to put numbers 1-4 on their individual whiteboard. In random order, read the four descriptions of prices and restrictions. Through careful listening, can the children write the correct ride's name next to its number on their whiteboard?

- Share experiences of theme parks. Which have the children visited? Have they been to any in Spanish-speaking countries? Mention *Parque de Atracciones*, a theme park on the western side of Madrid. Investigate its website on www.parquedeatracciones.es

- Suggest that the children could design their own theme park. Display and translate a copy of the planning sheet, photocopiable 23A. (How much is a ticket? How much for a family? Which rides? Minimum height? Minimum age? Opening times? How many cafés and restaurants? The park's name?)

- Put the children into groups of four.

Follow-up
Display useful reference material: ride names; a copy of the planning sheet with English translations; your model answers. Encourage group discussion as the children complete their own planning sheets for a theme park. Suggest choosing the park's name later - perhaps after researching names of Spanish cartoon characters. Listen to feedback from each group. Save the plans.

Lesson 2 ¡Era fantástico! (It was fantastic!)

Resources:
Pictures of theme-park rides; a computer and internet access; completed copies of photocopiable 23A (from 'Follow-up, Lesson 1)

- Speaking in the past tense, tell the children about your previous weekend: *En fin de semana pasado fui al parque de atracciones. ¡Era fantástico! Había una montaña rusa. ¡Era enorme! Había también un tren fantasma. ¡Era rápido y espantoso! Mi atracción favorita era el tiovivo. ¡Era lente!* (Last weekend, I went to the theme park. It was fantastic! There was a rollercoaster. It was enormous! There was also a ghost train. It was fast and frightening! My favourite ride was the merry-go-round. It was slow!)

- Repeat your oral description. Emphasise the verbs. Explain *fui*. Ask about *Había* and *era*. What do they mean? What tense are they? (Past)

- Put the children into groups of four for the memory game **Carriages**, but have a class practice first. The first person says *Fui al parque de atracciones y había… una montaña rusa.* The second person in the group repeats the sentence and adds a theme park ride (a 'carriage'). The next child repeats the extended sentence and adds a third ride. The fourth child has to remember and say everything and add a ride.

- Make sketches of the four rides from Lesson 1. Ask the children to identify them.

- Without speaking, write these adjectives on the whiteboard: *fantástico, enorme, rápido, espantoso, emocionante, extraordinario, gracioso, lente*.

- Put the children into pairs of television newsreaders. Their pronunciation matters! Can they offer each other strategies for pronouncing the words correctly?

- Share pronunciation tips: splitting words into syllables; identifying familiar graphemes; thinking of familiar words with the same ending.

- Read the words together.

- Tell the children your favourite weekend ride. *Mi atracción favorita era el tiovivo porque era lente.* Suggest they think of their last visit to a theme park and tell a partner what their favourite ride was, using the same sentence construction. Invite individuals to tell the class.

- Make another virtual visit to *Parque de Atracciones de Madrid* (www.parquedeatracciones.es) and investigate more of the rides and entertainment. What do the children most like the look of?

Follow-up
Re-form the planning groups (**Follow-up** Lesson 1). Let groups refresh their memories and decide how to share the work: for example, one child makes and writes about just one ride.

Lesson 3 El tren fantasma (The ghost train)

Resources:
Picture of a ghost train ride

- Put the children into pairs and display a picture of a ghost train ride.

- Ask the children to imagine being on this ride in a dark tunnel. Using a bilingual dictionary, let partners list three or four things they might see or hear.

- Write some on the whiteboard: *las cadenas* (chains); *un búho* (an owl); *una risa* (a laugh); *una bruja* (a witch); *un lobo* (a wolf);

- Agree on a mime for each and practise the vocabulary: you say the noun and the children mime; you mime and the children say the noun.

- Tell the children they are ghost train passengers. Suggest they close their eyes. The scary ride is about to start!

- Speak this commentary, the children reacting with their faces and body language:

> *Es de noche. El tren fantasma se pone en camino. Sshh. ¡Escuchad! ¿Qué es eso? ¿Es un búho? ¡Escuchad! ¿Qué es eso? ¿Es una rata? ¡Escuchad! ¿Qué es eso? ¿Es un lobo? Sí, es un lobo muy grande. ¡Escuchad! ¿Qué es eso? ¡Es una risa espantosa! Es la bruja misteriosa. ¡Ella viene!*
>
> (It's dark. The ghost train is starting to move off. Sshh. What's that?
> Is it an owl? Listen! What's that? Is it a rat? Listen! What's that? Is it a wolf? Yes it's a very big wolf. Listen! What's that? It's a frightening laugh! It's the mysterious witch. She's coming!)

- Explain your commentary and choose children to act as the chorus, responsible for the sound effects. Give them name cards so they can plan what noise to make.

- Warn the class to close their eyes again as the train ride re-starts. Speak your commentary, indicating to members of the chorus when to make their sounds. Heighten the atmosphere by playing appropriate music: *Danse macabre* (Saint-Saëns) would be very appropriate.

- Introduce the verbs *Monté, Vi, Oí*. Explain that they are past tense verbs and model their use: for example, *Monté en el tren fantasma. Vi un esqueleto. Oí las cadenas.* (I went for a ride on the ghost train. I saw a skeleton. I heard chains.)

Follow-up
Let the children tell a partner what they heard or saw when they were on a ghost train (a true or fictional account). Ask them to use your model to write about and illustrate a ghost train trip they made. Leave a bank of vocabulary on display.
Let the groups ('Follow-up' Lesson 1) continue creating their theme parks.

Lesson 4 El fin de semana pasado… (Last weekend…)

Resources:
Pictures of theme-parks; individual copies of photocopiable 23B

- Keep this text unseen by the children as you read it aloud:

- *El fin de semana pasado fui al parque de atracciones. ¡Era fantástico! Había una montaña rusa. ¡Era enorme! Había también un tren fantasma. ¡Era rápido y espantoso! Vi un esqueleto. Oí las cadenas. Mi atracción favorita era el tiovivo. ¡Era lento!*

- Put the children into pairs with a copy of photocopiable 23B. Ask them to cut the page into its nine separate sentences and order them.

- Suggest partners read their ordered text to each other. Which version makes most sense? What does the text mean?

- Display and order the text on the whiteboard. (You could drag-and-drop text on an interactive whiteboard.) Enlist the children's help, identifying words and phrases that show the text is about the past. (*El fin de semana pasado; fui; Era; Había; Vi*)

- Explain that this is the postcard you are sending home about your trip.

- Remove most of the text from the whiteboard, but retain its opening and important starters. For example:

    El fin de semana pasado, fui al parque de atracciones.
    Era…
    Había…
    Oí…
    Mi atracción favorita era…

- Use this writing frame to model write a different postcard. Afterwards leave just the opening and starters on the whiteboard.

- Let the children, in pairs, write a postcard about their visit to a theme park. Make sure there is a bank of helpful vocabulary on display.

Follow-up

Suggest partners 'post' their card to another pair of children. Do the readers understand it?
Let the groups from Lesson 1 complete their theme parks and rehearse their presentation to the class.

Parque de Atracciones

Parque de Atracciones is a very popular theme park on the western side of Madrid. Its most famous ride is El Abismo, a spectacular roller-coaster.

Un parque de atracciones

1. ¿Cuánto cuesta una entrada?

2. ¿Cuánto cuesta para una familia?

3. ¿Qué atracciones?

4. ¿Estatura mínima?

5. ¿Edad mínima?

6. ¿Los horarios?

7. ¿Cuántas cafeterías y cuántos restaurantes?

8. ¿El nombre del parque?

Fui al parque de atracciones

¡Era extraordinario!

¡Era enorme!

Mi atracción favorita era el tiovivo.

Vi un esqueleto y oí las cadenas.

Había también un tren fantasma.

Había también una noria.

¡Era lente!

El fin de semana pasado, fui al parque de atracciones.

Era rápido y emocionante.

More ideas for...

Work at school

- Use the work from **Follow-up** Lesson 1 as an on-going task for this unit. Encourage groups to think of innovative ways to display and advertise their theme parks. Let them research Spanish books for popular cartoon or fiction characters. These could inspire names for the theme parks and their rides.

- Give the children this simple script for buying tickets for a ride. Playing the scene in pairs, one child could be the ticket-seller, one the customer:

    A: *Una entrada para la noria, por favor.* (A ticket for the Big Wheel, please.)
    B: *Sí, eso es de nueve euros.* (Yes, that's nine euros.)
    A: *Gracias.* (Thank you.)

- Encourage the children to improvise by changing the price, the ride and the number of tickets.

- Create a class display of the postcards made in Lesson 4. Ask the children to identify the past tense verbs and the adjectives used.

Work at home

- Give the children a list of some of the adjectives used: *fantástico; emocionante; rápido; lente; espantoso; extraordinario* and their meanings. Ask the children to learn their meanings and spellings. Suggest this will be easier if they create calligrams (the words are drawn in a way that represents their meaning – for example, the letters in *rápido* could all have roller skates on.)

- Ask the children to check their information about euros. Can they convert them into sterling? Suggest they make a dual currency price list for four rides at their theme park: in euros and sterling.

- Suggest the children see what they can find out about age restrictions at a theme park in this country. How do they compare with ones in Spain? Are there many rides they would be too young for?

A Disney theme park may be coming to Spain! The planners want it to be built in Murcia, Spain. Your favourite Disney character will be there!

Unit 24 – Qué noticias hay?

(What's in the news?)

Unit theme
The news

Teaching points
- Making statements about newspaper columns
- Expressing and justifying opinions (using *porque en mi opinion*)

Grammar
- Using the possessive adjective: *mi, su*
- Replying to questions with *porque*

Language sounds
- Phoneme-grapheme correspondence

Vocabulary

la sección del tiempo	the weather column
la sección de moda	the fashion column
la sección de cocina	the cookery column
la sección de deportes	the sports column
Es interesante / precioso/demasiado largo	It is interesting / beautiful/too long
porque en mi/su opinión	as/since in my/his/her opinion
porque	because
la actualidad	current events

Additional vocabulary for teachers

el periódico/los periódicos	the newspaper/newspapers
una encuesta	a survey
¿por qué?	why?

Resources
Juan, the class puppet

¡Uno, dos, tres!

Lesson 1 Es interesante (It is interesting)

Resources:
A Spanish newspaper or access to a Spanish on-line newspaper; individual copies of photocopiable 24A

- Hold group and then class discussions in English about news. Pose discussion questions: What is 'news'? How do you find it out? Are newspapers useful?

- Explain that newspapers are divided into sections and columns: for example, weather.

- Put the children into pairs. Give them a copy of photocopiable 24A. Explain that the pictures represent the five columns listed. Can the children label them? Encourage partner discussion about strategies for working out meanings. What about pronunciation? Do they know words with the same ending or a familiar grapheme?

- Share pronunciation and meaning strategies before you show answers on the whiteboard and say the column names for the children to repeat.

- Show the children a paper or online Spanish newspaper from www.onlinenewspapers.com/spain.htm Can they find *la sección del tiempo, la sección de moda, la sección de cocina, la sección de actualidad* and *la sección de deportes*. Can they identify others? How?

- Without reading them aloud, write these six phrases on the whiteboard: *Es genial/interesante/ aburrido/ fantástico/precioso/ demasiado largo* (It's brilliant/interesting/boring/fantastic/beautiful/too long).

- Put the children into groups of four, each child with a piece of card. Ask the children to write a phrase from the whiteboard, each group member choosing a different one.

- Suggest the groups use dictionaries and sort their cards into positive and negative comments. Encourage breaking words into segments and using their experience of phoneme–grapheme correspondence to work out pronunciation.

- Let the groups compare their sorting results with another group. Do they agree? Share answers as a class. Do the children know any other words for expressing an opinion?

- Are any phrases from the whiteboard still unplaced? Which type are they?

Follow-up
Opinion Bingo Call out a phrase. If groups own it, they wave it in the air and set it aside. The first group to set aside all their phrases calls 'House!'

Up/down Say an opinion phrase in a positive or negative way. If your manner of speaking matches the phrase's meaning, the children should give a thumbs up. If your voice does not match, they give a thumbs down. (For example, *Es fantástico* said in a negative way gets a thumbs down.) Owners of the wrong thumbs are out!

Lesson 2 En mi opinión (In my opinion)

Resources:
The class puppet; individual copies of photocopiable 24B

- Return to the newspaper columns from Lesson 1. Play **Pictogram**: call out a column's name for the children to draw an appropriate picture on their individual whiteboard.

- Display these five column names: *la sección del tiempo, la sección de moda, la sección de cocina, la sección de actualidad, la sección de deportes.*

- Put the children into pairs or small groups. Give out copies of photocopiable 24B.

- Allow reading time. Encourage identifying familiar words to gain a gist of what the text is about. Are some other meanings easily guessed? (*infectados, contagioso*)

- Ask the children general questions, in English, about the content.

- Point to the column headings. Where should this article go? (*la sección de actualidad.*)

- Write two sentences on the whiteboard: *Me gusta la sección de deportes. Es interesante.* Ask about the meaning. (I like the sports column. It's interesting.)

- Let the children use the same two-sentence pattern to tell their partner:

  ○ which column they like (*Me gusta…*) or dislike (*No me gusta…*);

  ○ why they like/dislike it (*Es…*).

- Listen to some of the children's sentences.

- Return to your two sentences on the whiteboard. Suggest linking them into one sentence. What connective do the children know? (*porque*) What other ones do they know in English? (for, as)

- Introduce the phrase *porque à mon avis* (as in my opinion). Demonstrate its use: *Me gusta la sección de actualidad porque en mi opinión es interesante.*

- Get out Juan, your class puppet. Ask: *¿Te gusta la sección de moda?* Let him answer *No, no me gusta la sección de moda porque en mi opinión es ridiculo.* (Do you like the fashion column? No, I don't like the fashion column as in my opinion it's ridiculous.) Give the children oral practice in using the connective phrase.

- Ask the children to choose and write down:

   ○ three newspaper columns;

   ○ three questions to ask people about liking those columns – for example, *¿Te gusta la seccion de cocina?*

Follow-up
Let the children conduct and save a newspaper survey, asking four children a question. Suggest they draw and write the person's name and record their answer in a speech bubble. (For example: *No, no me gusta la sección de actualidad porque en mi opinión es demasiado largo.*)

Lesson 3 En su opinion (In his/her opinion)

Resources:
A computer and large display screen (preferably an interactive whiteboard); the children's surveys from **Follow-up** Lesson 2

- Put the children into small groups and set a timed challenge: to write down the names of the five newspaper columns. (If necessary, provide visual clues or initial letters.)

- Return the surveys done in **Follow–up** Lesson 2. Display part of your own survey:

   ○ a question: *¿Te gusta la sección de moda?* and a picture of Juan;

   ○ a speech bubble containing his answer: *No, no me gusta la sección de moda porque en mi opinión es ridículo.*

- Point out the possessive adjective *mi*. What does it mean? (my) Ask the children to find *mi* in the answers they were given.

   ○ Remove your display, explaining that you prefer to tell them about Juan. Say and write *Juan no le gusta la sección de moda porque en su opinión es ridículo.*

- Do the children spot a change? Why has *mi* become *su*? (*su* is the third person possessive adjective meaning his or her). Give the children another example sentence.

- Put the children into small groups. Using their surveys, but not displaying them, they should report to one another some children's opinions. Encourage them to help one another to use *su* instead of *mi*. Let some children report to the class.

- Now tell the children your exciting idea: a newspaper in which the children will write about themselves: their likes, dislikes and plans for the future.

- Form writing groups of about four children to plan and write an introductory paragraph. This will form the first page of the newspaper. Ask them to write: that it is the end of the school year; that the class is leaving; the name of the class; where they will be going in September; what this newspaper is about.

- Display some helpful phrases, perhaps from the example text below.

Follow-up
Share results. Work as a class, forming, improving and ordering sentences. Use a computer, with the agreed text displayed on an interactive whiteboard. For example:

¡Hola! Es julio y es el fin del año escolar. ¡El año 6 va terminar el colegio! En septiembre los alumnos van al instituto. En nuestro periódico escolar, puede informarse sobre los alumnos.

(Hello! It's July and the end of the school year. Year 6 is leaving the school! In September the children are going to secondary school. In our school newspaper, you can find out all about the children.) Save your text.

Lesson 4 El periódico escolar (The school newspaper)

Resources:
Individual copies of the planning questionnaire shown; individual access to computers

- Remind the children about their class newspaper and the introduction written (**Follow-up** Lesson 4). Now they have to write their personal articles.

- Give everyone this planning questionnaire to write answers:

    ¿Cómo te llamas? (What are you called?)
    ¿Cuántos años tienes? (How old are you?)
    ¿Tienes un hermano o una hermana?
    (Do you have a brother or sister?)
    ¿Te gusta la música? (Do you like music?)
    ¿Dónde vives? (Where do you live?)
    ¿Juegas al fútbol? (Do you play football?)

- Display Juan's written answers: *Yo me llamo Juan. Tengo diez años. Tengo una hermana. Me gusta la música. Vivo en Londres. Si, juego al fútbol.*

- Demonstrate how Juan uses his planning answers to help him create a text:

    ¡Hola! Yo me llamo Juan. Tengo diez años. Tengo una hermana. Ella tiene ocho años. Me gusta mucho la música porque en mi opinión la música es fantástica. Vivo en Londres. Juego al fútbol y el golf. Me gustaría ser futbolista.

- Point out that Juan has sometimes added detail to his original answers. Highlight and explain the last sentence. (I would like to become a footballer.) Ask everyone to add this *Me gustaría ser... (profesor)* (...a teacher) to their planning sheet.

- Suggest they write the final word on their individual whiteboard and draw a picture. Holding the boards up, the children should group themselves into newspaper columns.

- Agree on the columns' names and list them under your newspaper's introduction.

Follow-up
Suggest the children write a draft version of their article for a partner to check, and then write or type the final version. An illustration – paper or electronic – will add interesting detail.

Collate the articles into both paper and electronic newspapers: visitors to the school will enjoy reading one in the entrance hall; users of the school's website will be delighted to find an online copy.

¡Uno, dos, tres!

Un periódico

la sección de cocina

la sección de actualidad

la sección del tiempo

la sección de deportes

la sección de moda

Es el Swine Flu

Un virus contagioso durante más de cinco días

Hay una terrible enfermedad en España. Es el Swine Flu. Muchos alumnos de las dos escuelas de Málaga están muy enfermos. Tres niños están en el hospital. Ellos están infectados por el virus H1N1. Un niño visitó México y estaba enfermo. Cuando regresó a Málaga, que era contagioso. Ahora, su escuela y la escuela de su hermana están cerrados por una semana. Todos los alumnos se quedan en casa.

Translation:

It's Swine Flu

Virus contagious for more than five days

There is a terrible illness in Spain. It's Swine Flu. Many pupils in two schools in Malaga are very ill. Three children are in hospital. They are infected by the virus H1N1. One boy visited Mexico and was ill. When he returned to Malaga, he was contagious. Now, his school and his sister's school are closed for a week. All the pupils are staying at home.

More ideas for...

Work at school

- Ask the children to list the adjectives in photocopiable 23B, Part 1 and to write their masculine, feminine and plural forms. Can they find examples of the third person singular possessive adjective in this text? (*su*)

- Commission the children, in pairs or small groups, to write an article about a new theme park or café in their town. Refresh their memories with a bank of useful vocabulary from Units 21 and 23.

- Make a display of the class's likes and dislikes. One half of the board can be headed **Me gusta...** the other half headed **No me gusta...** Let the children draw self-portraits and speech bubbles with information about their likes or dislikes.

- Give the children opportunities to look at online Spanish newspapers. Can they understand the headlines? What interesting news do they manage to find out?

- Play oral games with **Por que?** (Why?) Let the children make statements expressing opinions. Encourage them to justify their opinions with *porque en mi opinion...*

Work at home

- Give the children a copy of photocopiable 23B, Part 1. Ask them to answer these comprehension questions in English. How good are their translation skills?

  Questions:
  1. What is the article about?
  2. Which section of the paper would you put it in?
  3. What is the name of the illness?
  4. How many schools are involved?
  5. Where are the schools?
  6. How many children are in hospital?
  7. Who started the illness in the schools?
  8. How long are the two schools closed?

- Suggest the children read part of an English newspaper every day for a week. Encourage them to read articles from different columns in the paper. At the end of the week, what do they have to report? In school, invite them to express opinions in Spanish about what they read, reporting to a partner or small group.

- Give the children a copy of the planning questionnaire used in Lesson 4. Ask the children to interview a family member and record their answers. Back at school, let them report some of the answers given, speaking in the third person: for example: *Mi madre no le gusta el deporte.*

The main Spanish newspapers are available in paper form and also online.

¡Uno, dos, tres!